LEE UFAN & CLAUDE VIALLAT

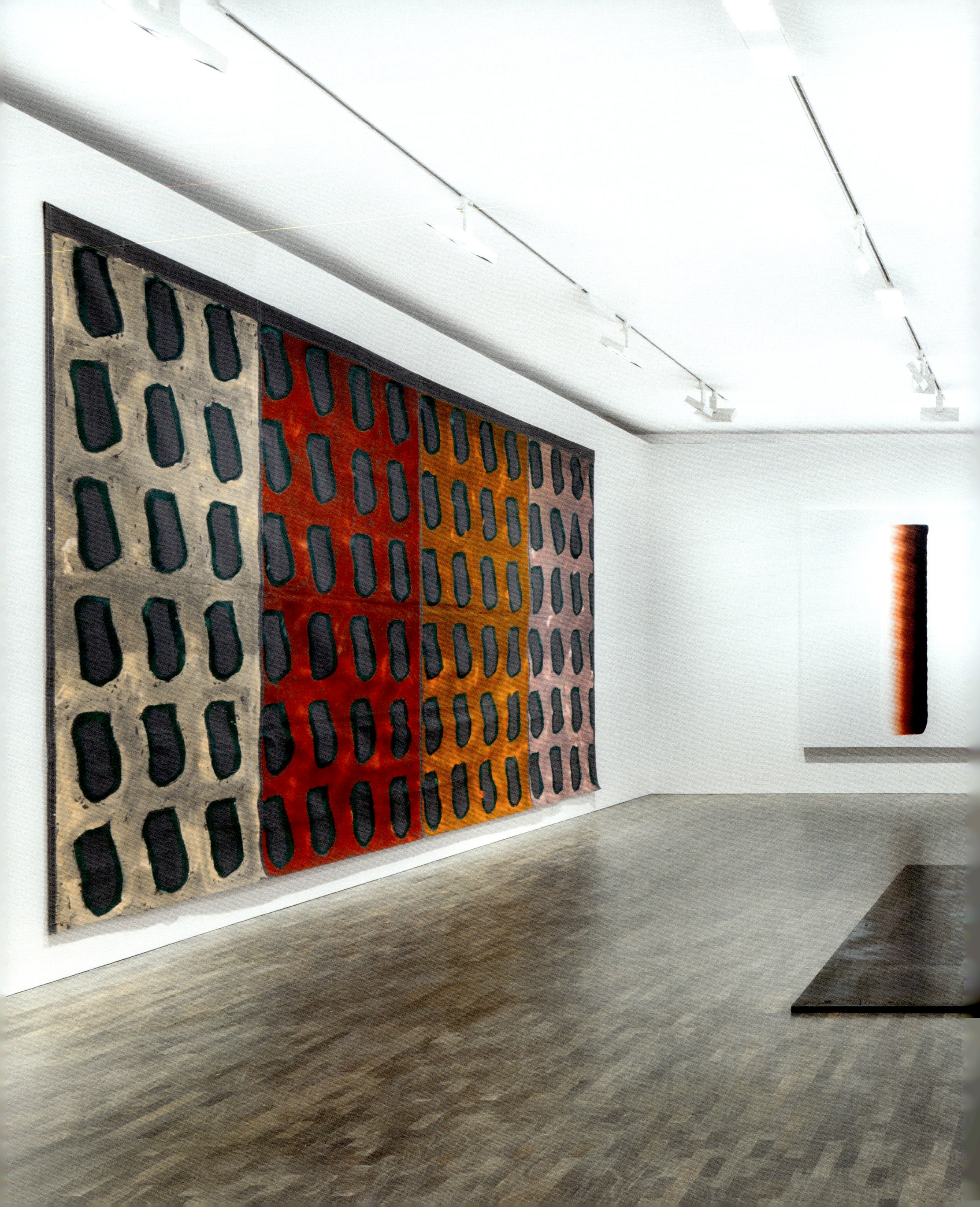

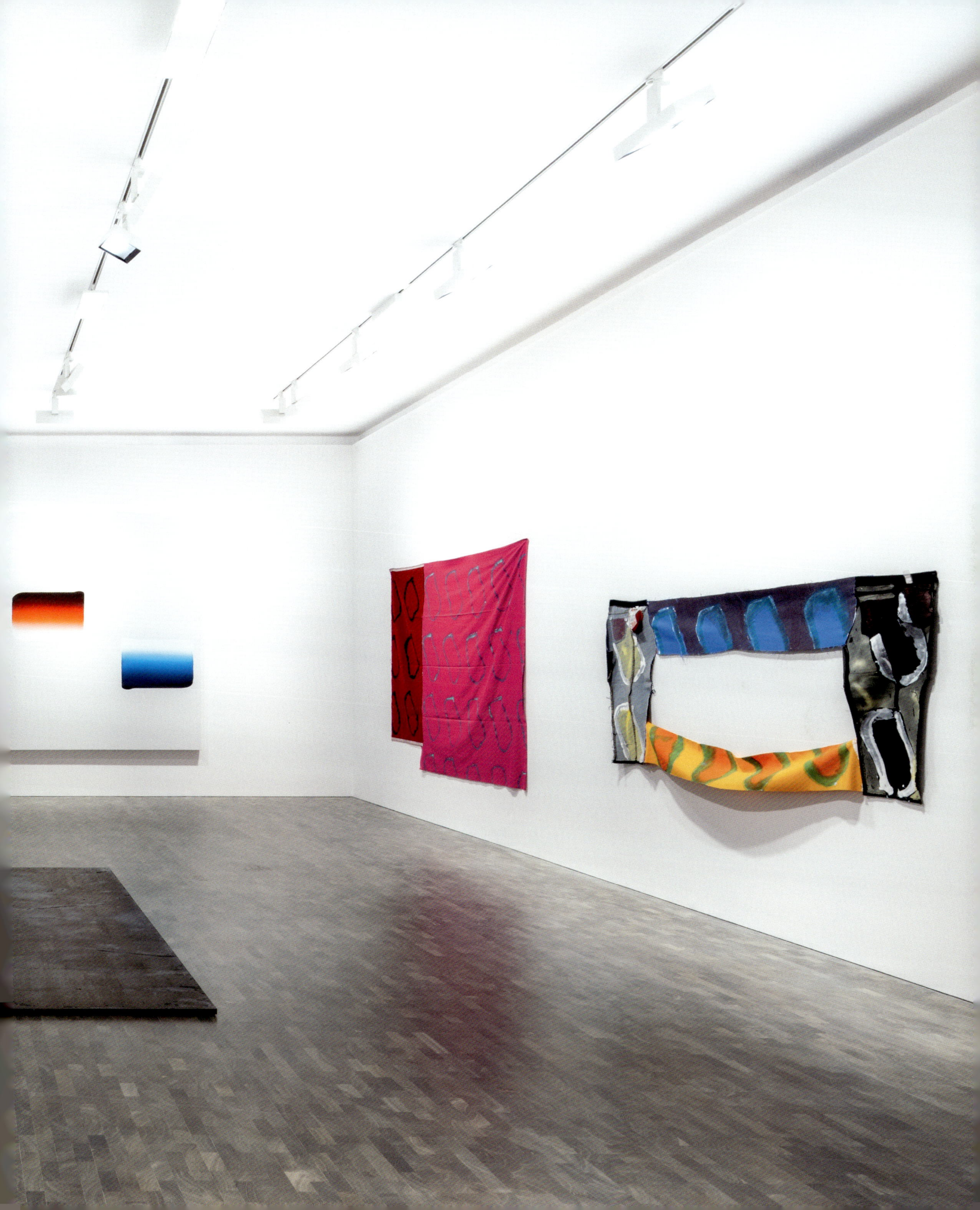

LEE UFAN & CLAUDE VIALLAT

Curated by Alfred Pacquement

PACE

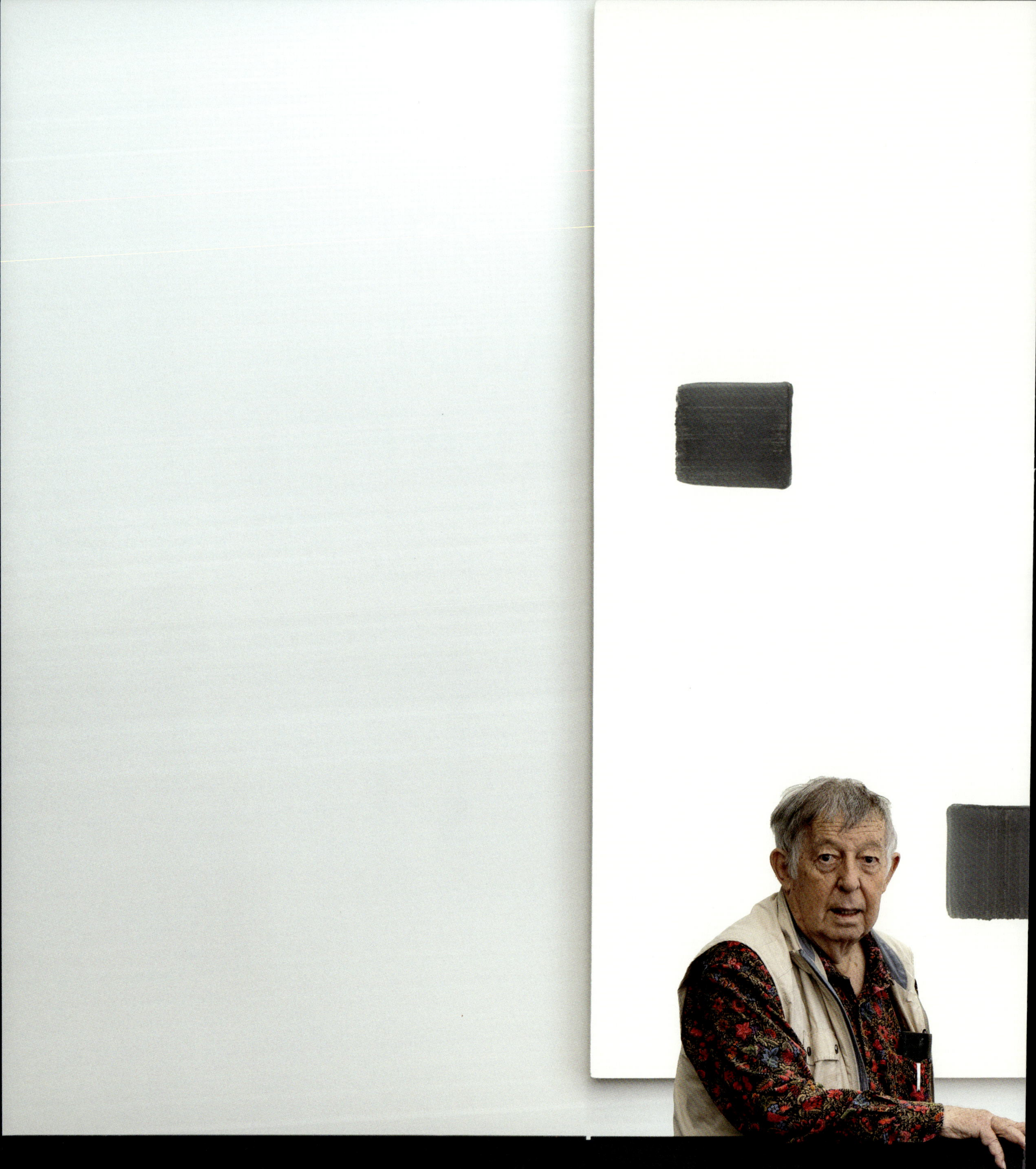

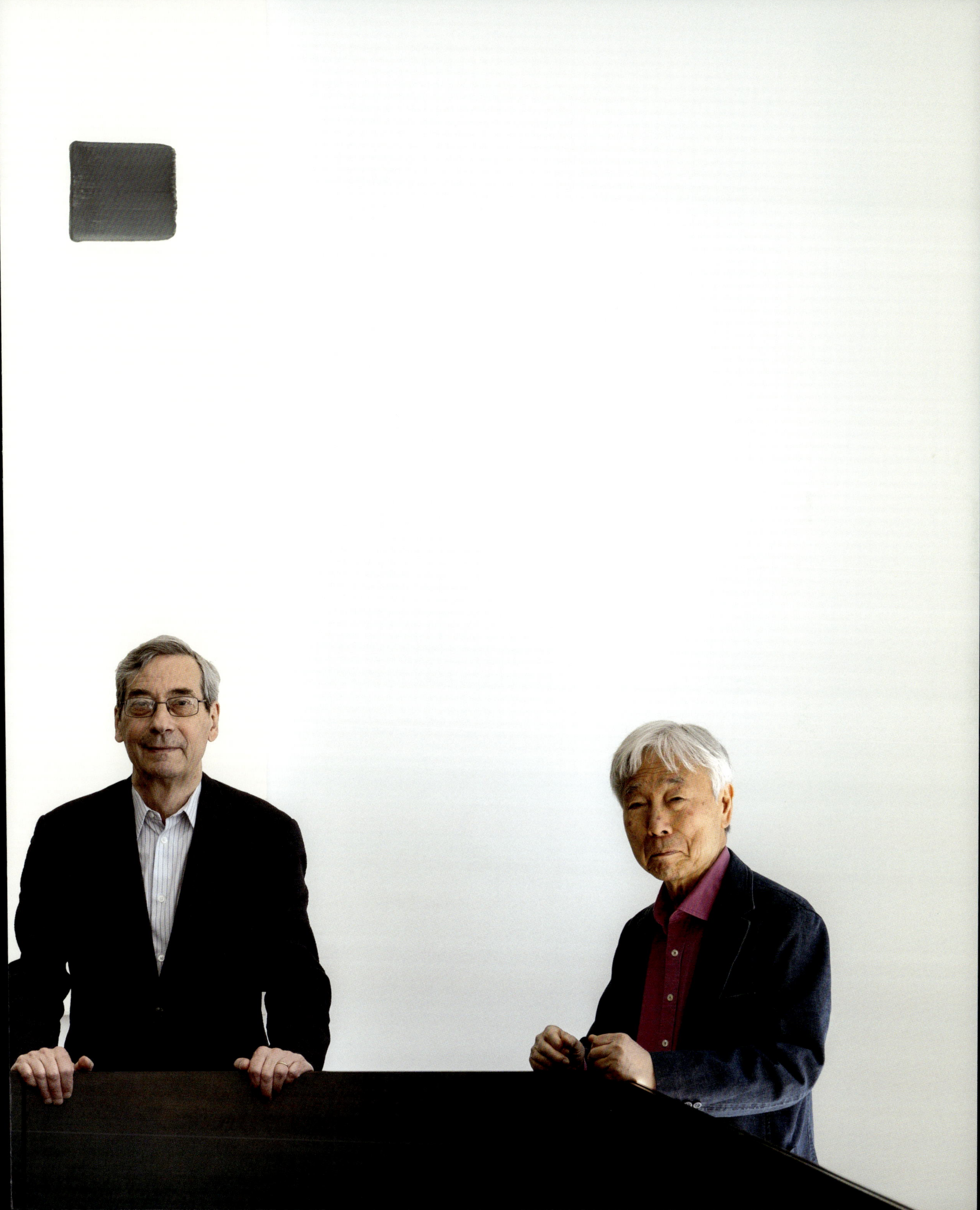

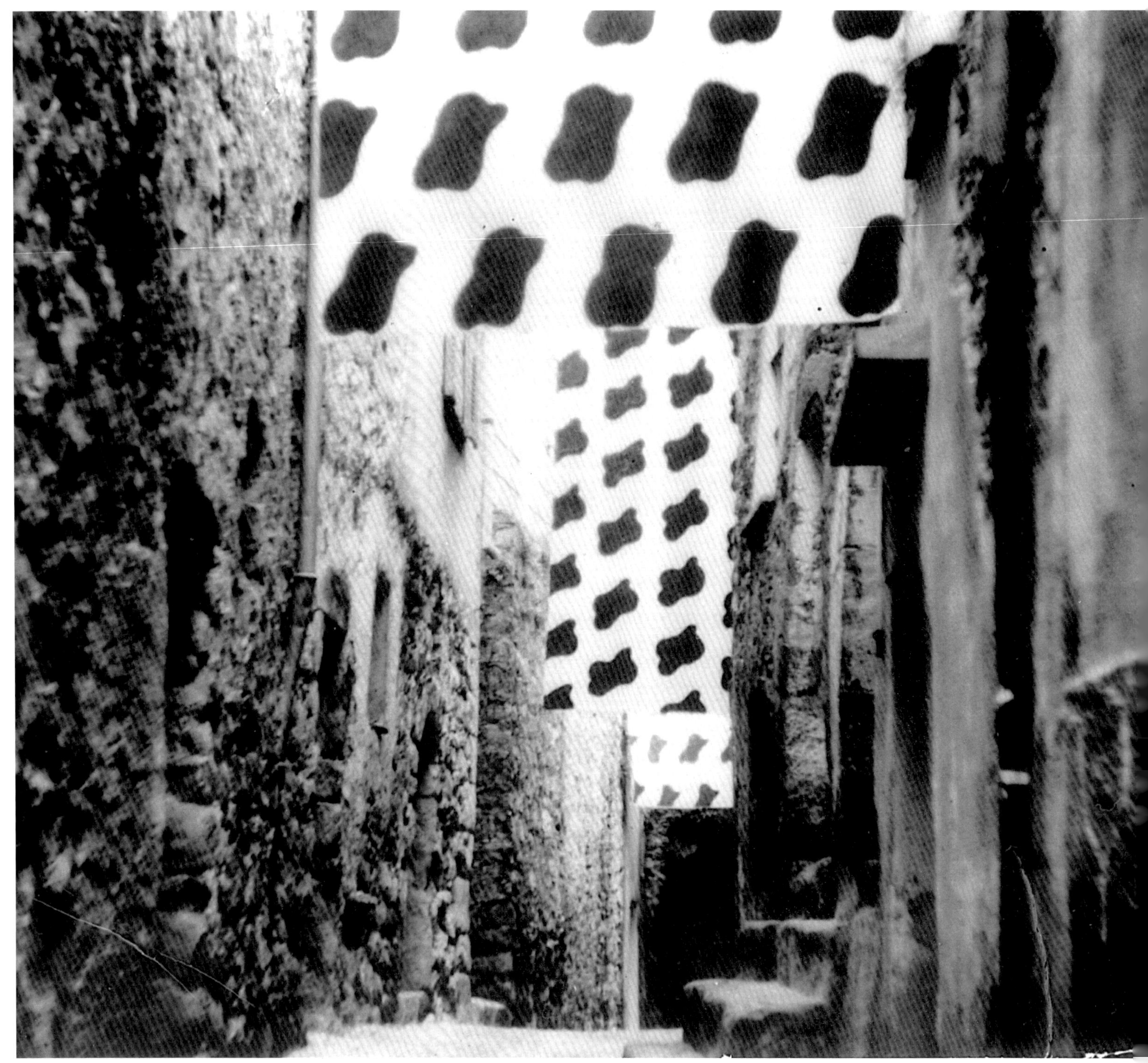

fig. 1
Claude Viallat
toile dans une ruelle, Coaraze, 1969

Alfred Pacquement

LEE UFAN AND CLAUDE VIALLAT:

AN ENCOUNTER

Lee Ufan and Claude Viallat were both born in 1936, a few weeks apart, very far away from each other, and in very different cultures. Their background, their history, and the starting points of their respective works are quite distinct. After receiving a classical education in his native Korea, which included poetry, calligraphy, and painting, Lee moved to Japan somewhat by chance at the age of 20 when he brought medicinal herbs to an uncle. This was when Korea, long under Japanese domination and then divided into two distinct enemy countries, experienced a devastating war and a series of authoritarian regimes. Lee then settled permanently in Japan and studied philosophy and art there. He began his mature work at the end of the 1960s, at the time of his first exhibitions. First, we see his sculptures combining different natural and industrial materials, followed a few years later by a series of abstract paintings based on repetitive brushstrokes. Subsequently, the two genres came to coexist in his work.

Viallat was born in Nîmes in the south of France, where he still lives today. He will always be strongly associated with his native region, the local cultures, and especially the bullfighting traditions. He studied art in Montpellier and then in Paris, interrupting his studies to complete his military service in France and then in Algeria. Quite early on, he began to teach in art schools. His first exhibitions took place in the second half of the 1960s in cultural venues as well as outdoor locations (see fig. 1). Canvases without frames, choosing a unique shape, but also mesh, knotted ropes, and driftwood, were incorporated into his vocabulary from the outset.

Within one or two years, the two artists found their paths at the same time, Viallat through an uninterrupted pictorial quest based on repeatedly using a shape, which has since maintained its relevance in his work, as well as his decision to use fabrics of all kinds as a support. These were often second-hand, sometimes oversized. He rejected the use of a frame, opening the door for all sorts of unconventional hanging devices. His works frequently featured objects made of found materials that were often fragile and pieced together. Lee's sculptures were conceived as an encounter between materials, like natural stones accompanied by glass or metal plates, but also highlighted the opposition between heavy stones and lighter materials, such as cotton, canvases, paper, etc (see fig. 2). Concurrently, he pursued painting, influenced by his discovery of the black-and-white canvases of Barnett Newman during his first trip to New York in 1971. His subsequent series consisted of brushstrokes filling the surface, then wide paint streaks, which gradually gave way to large sections of white canvas.

The two artists met at the Biennale de Paris in the fall of 1971, where their works cohabited for the first time. Viallat took part in the exhibition as part of the Supports/Surfaces movement with a huge canvas. Meanwhile, the nascent group was already beginning to disintegrate, with some artists opting for a political statement rather than exhibiting their pictorial studies.[1] Lee was traveling to Europe for the first time for this event. He was invited to participate in this exhibition as part of the Korean selection with several works representing his sculptural approach. Several Japanese artists then associated with the Mono-ha movement also participated in this exhibition.[2] Even though Lee had no discussions with Viallat on this occasion, he could not have missed the free canvas that Viallat had hung in the exhibition space. He would later say how impressed he was. Viallat, in turn, had observed the works of the Mono-ha artists with great interest during the previous Biennial in 1969, where he also participated.[3] Thus, the formal and intellectual relationship between the two artists, as well as between the two groups with which they were associated, was in the air at the time, and their meeting was a natural outcome.

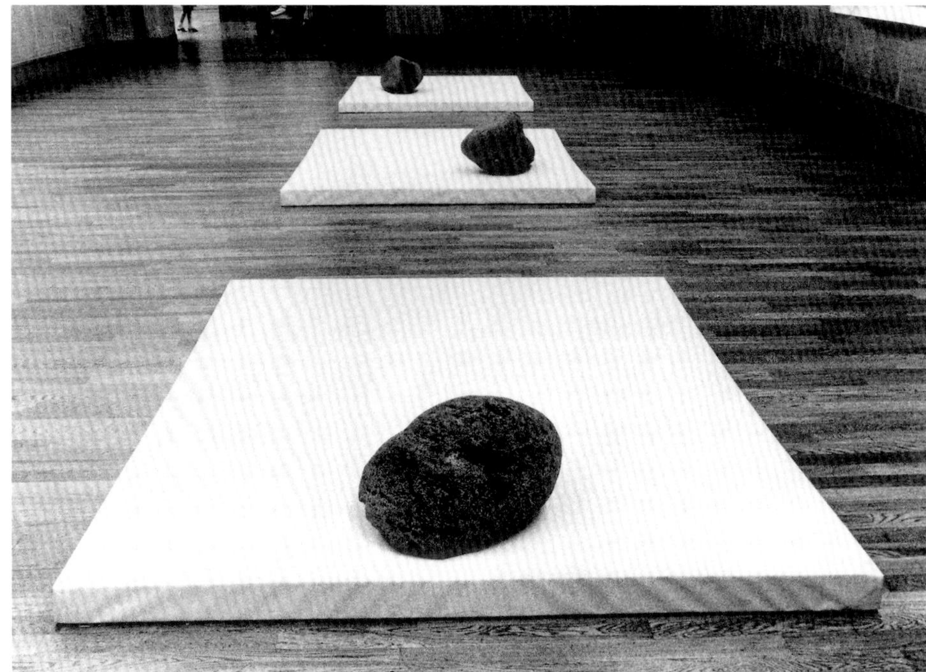

fig. 2
Lee Ufan
installation view: 10th Contemporary Art Exhibition of Japan: *Man and Nature*, Tokyo Metropolitan Art Museum, May 10–30, 1971

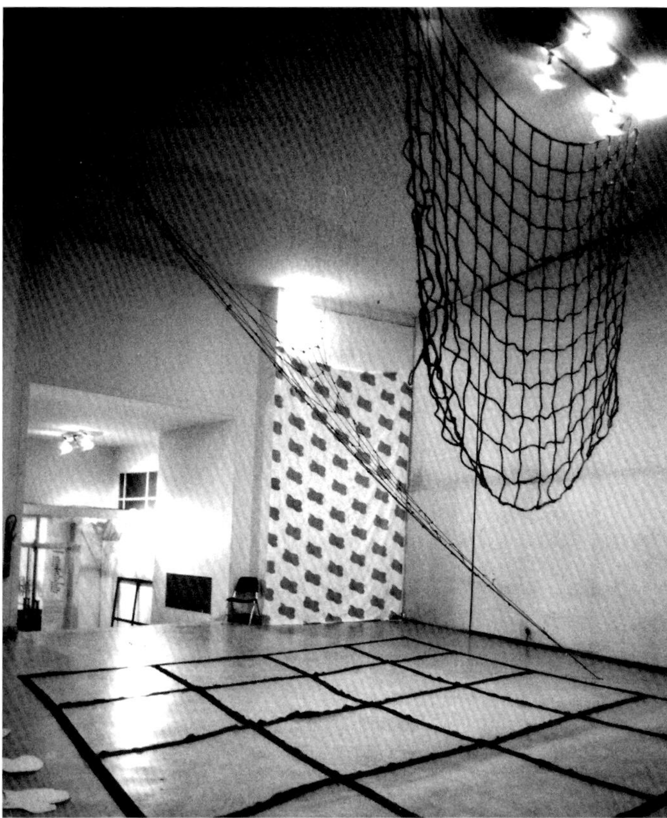

fig. 3
Vincent Bioulès, Patrick Saytour,
André Valensi, Claude Viallat
installation view: *Supports/Surfaces*, ARC 1,
Musée d'Art Moderne, Paris, September 1970

Supports/Surfaces is the name of a group of artists founded in 1970, whose duration as a group was as short-lived as its impact on the art scene in France was decisive (see fig. 3). Its contribution to a reconsideration of painting and its components, the freedom that the artists demanded to dispose of the support/canvas, which could, for example, be detached from its frame and float in space, as well as the desire to reconnect with abstract practices following a decade dominated by the object and the image, fomented the emergence of a new generation of painters. They would profoundly impact the 1970s and beyond with this ambition to demystify the object-painting. The short history of Supports/Surfaces was, however, shaken by various upheavals and conflicts among the artists participating in the group's exhibitions. The political situation was in a period of extremes, coming shortly after the events of 1968, when student demonstrations expanded to the whole working class and then to a general strike threatening to topple the government. Many artists had been involved in these events, occupying the École des Beaux-Arts in Paris and creating many famous posters with overt slogans. The militancy exhibited by some, but also the divergent aesthetics, contributed to dividing the group.

Although the Supports/Surfaces name appeared in 1970, the activities and works of the those involved began a few years earlier. Even before the group was founded, exhibitions had cited the collaborative contributions of the artists, living for the most part in the south of France, in questioning the classical attributes of painting. Initiated by the artists themselves and often mounted in unusual places like beaches or on the streets of towns or villages, these events sought—to borrow from one of their titles—"to question painting." Viallat produced his first paintings on free canvas in 1966, with his study of form being reduced to the repetition of the motif that would become his trademark and to the vagaries of recovered supports, allowing for a continual renewal of his work while emphasizing color.

Approximately ten artists were associated with Supports/Surfaces, although the list changed from one exhibition to another. The first event under this name at the Musée d'Art Moderne de Paris (Animation, Recherche, Confrontation division, ARC) took place in September 1970 and included six artists: Vincent Bioulès, Marc Devade, Daniel Dezeuze, Patrick Saytour, André Valensi, and Viallat. It was Bioulès who suggested the name, which was to be a landmark. Viallat has noted that the exhibition was to have taken place the previous year, but the ARC curator, Pierre Gaudibert, did not want Marcelin Pleynet, an influential critic at the time who was close to some of the artists, involved. And so the exhibition took place without his collaboration. For the next event at the Cité Universitaire de Paris in April 1971, the group was enlarged to include four guests: André-Pierre Arnal, Louis Cane, Noël Dolla, and Jean-Pierre Pincemin. Two months later, at the Théâtre de Nice, the group appeared with an additional artist, Toni Grand, the only sculptor to have been associated with it for a short time. Two factions quickly emerged: "provincials" versus Parisians. During the intervening time, the group had experienced its first divisions with the resignation of Viallat a few months earlier, followed by the departure of several other artists. And in September, on the occasion of the seventh Biennale de Paris (in which Lee participated, as mentioned), only Viallat and Dolla exhibited their works, while the citation of the Supports/Surfaces group included Arnal, Bioulès, Cane, Devade, Dezeuze, and Pincemin and was presented under the title of "Supports/Surfaces: Peinture-Cahiers théoriques." A magazine was published under this name in the summer of 1971, at the prompting of some of the artists mentioned above, ideologically similar to the magazine *Tel Quel*[4] and strongly exhibiting pro-Chinese political sentiments that were in vogue at the time. Other resignations followed. The rupture was complete.

Beyond the quarrels fueled by vicious pamphlets, resignations, and the almost immediate break-up of the nascent group, it was the very shared issues and differences of the members of Supports/Surfaces and a few other painters in their inner circle that made this "moment," to use Bernard Ceysson's term, an essential stage in the recent history of abstract painting.[5] Supports/Surfaces undeniably has its place among these movements that marked an upheaval in artistic approaches at the beginning of the 1970s. And even if the group as such did not last long, and its impact was limited to France at that time, its name remains strongly present in memory, and now it is part of the history of art.

For Viallat, and for most of the group's members, reflection on the status of painting, on the pictorial, fueled by the contributions of post-war American abstract painting—which then had little presence in France other than through reproductions in books and magazines—was at the heart of the process.

> Claude Viallat: *"Reading Nikolaï Tarabukin's* Le Dernier Tableau (The Last Painting)[6] *was very important. We misinterpreted Jackson Pollock's position because we thought Pollock was painting on the canvas and not from the edges. So if we put canvases on the ground and*

walked on them, we thought at that time (with the idea we had of the United States, of oversized American paintings) that we could paint on the ground directly on the canvas. This liberated us on all sides. In other words, we no longer had the horizon line, and, at the same time, the concept of a painting was shattered.

Another very important reference was Le Geste et la Parole (Gesture and Speech) *by André Leroi-Gourhan.*[7] *This book made us think about the art of origins or the origins of art and, at the same time, allowed us to couple the history of painting with the history of civilizations, with the manufacture of objects. So we reintegrated artifacts into the history of art and into the history of painting. If art was finished, it had to start over and it had to start over in a different way. In other words, we had to try to think of it in a completely different way. And for painting (since that was what it was all about for us), what provided the setting for the painting was the canvas, or the canvas stretched on a frame with interacting tensions.*

We realized that when we exhibited together, Daniel Dezeuze worked on frames without canvas, I worked on canvases without frames, and Patrick Saytour used the image of the frame on the canvas. This was when we began to reflect on the deconstruction of the painting and then on the deconstruction of all the elements that made up the painting, in other words, both the woven material and the wood, soft materials and hard materials, etc. And the image was only a result of accepting all its realities. What was most important was, in a way, to reject a return to imagery and themes, which, in the end, some of the group did not accept at all. Still, it was action that dominated, and the painting was always seen as the result of action and accepted as such. Practice preceded theory, rather than the other way around. The situation of Supports/Surfaces was complicated because we had decided to exhibit in unlikely spaces—outside, in places not intended for exhibitions—and to install or hang pieces when it was possible in these places, leaving them as they were, at the mercy of passers-by.

However, other members of Supports/Surfaces continued to work with the frame on traditional elements, paying much more attention to color and the distribution of color on the canvas. In addition, some lived in Paris and worked under the control, under the whip, of the magazine Tel Quel, *unlike the others living in the provinces. There was a very big divide there."*

Unlike Supports/Surfaces, Mono-ha is not an established group but an ex-post-facto designation recognizing a certain homogeneity in the work of a dozen Japanese artists of the same generation, all born during the years of World War II and starting to exhibit around 1970. Lee, who was a little older than these young artists from the same university who came together for a few exhibitions or publications, would quickly be considered an essential figure for them. Very early on, he wrote texts, which identified him as the theoretician of the movement. It should be added that the term Mono-ha, which can be translated as "The School of Things," is a qualifier of a negative, even pejorative tendency, which was nevertheless adopted by the members as a label for their group.

Everything began with a series of events, exhibitions in Tokyo, and articles in the Japanese press in 1970, the same year the Supports/Surfaces group emerged in France. This means that the two collectives have a remarkable simultaneity.

Post-war artists in Japan tended to rally around an older artist, and many groups followed one after another during the 1950s and 1960s, creating a blank slate freed from the past and emphasizing performance, anti-art, and Neo-Dada. We should mention Gutai following Yoshihara Jirō, Jikken kōbō following Shūzō Takiguchi, and later Neo-Dada organizers following Yoshimura Masunobu. Mono-ha reinvented a sculptural approach and emerged as a "group of artists who use natural or industrial materials almost in their raw state . . . which they simply juxtapose in temporary, interdependent arrangements to observe the relationship between the materials, as well as the nature of their respective state within these relationships."[8]

> Lee Ufan: *"In Japan, as in France, this period was one of protest and social movements. It was a time when we truly saw everything that had been gained with modernity crumble. So we were looking for new starting points. From the intellectual standpoint, this period was symbolized by the term 'deconstruction.' Unlike what came before, which always positioned itself in relation to traditional art by seeking to destroy what had existed before, we were really freed from the art that had come before, and we wanted to find a new context that would give us a fresh start.*
>
> *For the members of Mono-ha, the important thing was the profound questioning of what seemed quite normal and ordinary for artists: the act of doing or painting. But even for these completely innocuous acts, we had to reexamine everything, ask ourselves what expression is and under what conditions we could really mount an exhibition. This was the starting point of the Mono-ha group."*

In 1970, numerous exhibitions in Tokyo and Kyoto, and several articles published in the Japanese press, brought together the artists who shaped this movement: Sekine Nobuo, Suga Kishio, Yoshida Katsuro, Narita Katsuhiko, and Koshimizu Susumu. They all met at Tama University in Tokyo. Lee was drawn to what was essentially the founding work of the Mono-ha movement, *Phase–Mother Earth*, by Sekine (fig. 4). He met Sekine and noted the convergence of their approach. Sekine's much-discussed involvement in an open-air sculpture exhibition in Kobe consisted of a large-scale cylinder of earth displayed alongside a cylindrical hole of the same volume dug into the ground.[9] Concurrently, Lee, who had begun exhibiting, designed his first sculpture of the Relatum series, which he continues to this day.

The beginnings of Mono-ha coincide with a discussion led by Lee, with the five artists mentioned above, published in a Japanese art magazine under the title "Mono Opens a New World."[10] That same year, Lee published a book titled *The Search for Encounter*, an essential companion to his theoretical thought fed by his philosophical readings, particularly those of Michel Foucault and Maurice Merleau-Ponty.

Lee Ufan: *"Certainly, among my works, some showed a kind of resistance or protest against the institution or the politics of the time. For example, cracked glass plates, with rocks placed on the surface. This somewhat symbolizes the act of destruction, demolition. And I wasn't the only one. Other Mono-ha artists had more or less the same approach.*

So I completely refused to paint. More specifically, I simply hung totally white canvases on the wall. I also placed several canvases on the ground without painting anything on them. Other artists have simply burned a wooden beam and then presented it as it is, raw, in an exhibition.[11] *All of this symbolized our desire for a clean slate. The act of making was questioned. Beginning from this really ambiguous situation, we very seriously questioned ourselves about what the genesis of our act should be. That's how Mono-ha artists worked back then. At that time, when I looked around us, I discovered the works of Arte Povera, Supports/Surfaces, Anti-form, and I realized that, at about the same time, we were pursuing ideas from similar thoughts that led to comparable results, which greatly surprised me. It was undoubtedly the first time in the history of art that, concurrently, in different geographical locations, analogous tendencies were born.*

In modernity, it was the artist who dominated, the artist who imposed everything, which stems from the ego. However, this kind of approach was destroyed with the disappearance of imperialism, of colonialism, and everything that had been built up was therefore shaken up

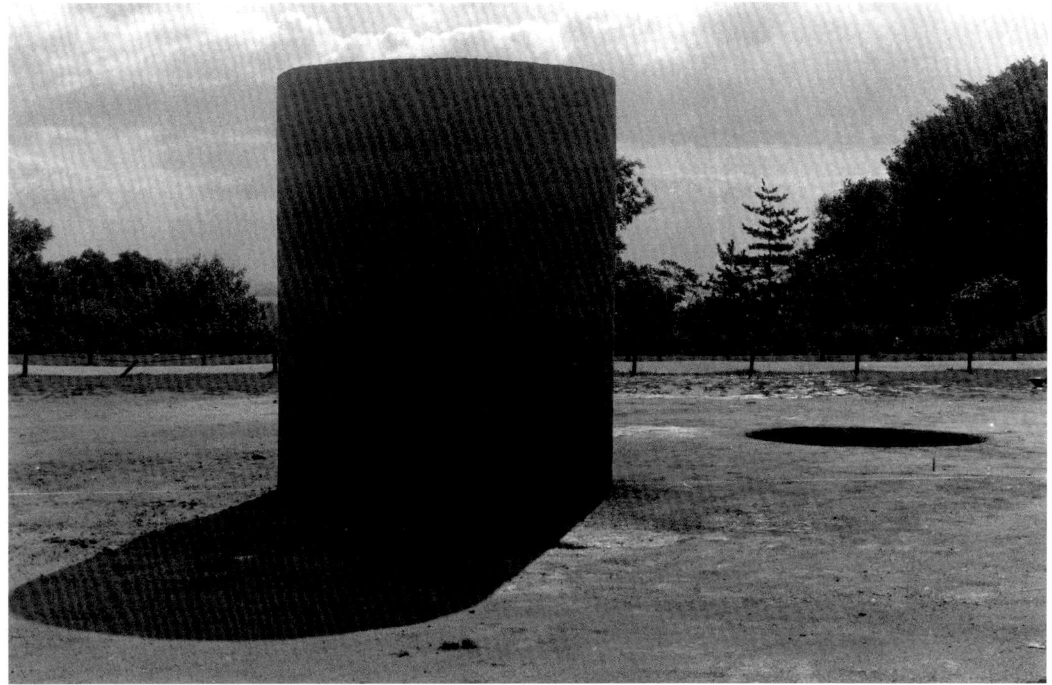

fig. 4
Sekine Nobuo
Phase—Mother Earth,
1st Kobe Suma Rikyū Park
Contemporary Sculpture
Exhibition, October 1 –
November 10, 1968

and dismantled. It was mainly French anthropologists and philosophers, Claude Lévi-Strauss, Michel Foucault, and Gilles Deleuze, who described this change. These thinkers were very popular in Japan. We became aware of this phenomenon and wanted to react against the sophistication of production imposed by modernity. There was a quest for a new beginning in different places around the world."

And today? Establishing a parallel between the work of Lee and that of Viallat stretches the boundaries of this type of comparison, which cannot be satisfied with formal similarities, because they are not really present in this case. The repetition of a broad brushstroke on an immaculate canvas in Lee's work has no equivalent in the ever-changing diversity of Viallat's use of a single form employing all sorts of techniques, generally using second-hand fabrics. The two artists' relationship to the exhibition space nevertheless has common implications, regardless of the differences in approach. Viallat can install his works in a variety of ways: hung in the middle of the room if they are painted on both sides, placed on the floor, hung from a single point, etc (see fig. 5). When he exhibits his works, Viallat "works" the space. There is studio time when the painter gathers available fabrics, and then there is hanging time: "I always approach the space as a whole, with the desire to occupy the ground as well as the walls. . . . I work with the space when I hang it. There is always a flow that makes one canvas respond to another, a shift of the gaze from one wall to another. There are canvases that I can put in several different positions. This circles back to my idea of demystification, which is extremely important. The canvas is above all a tactile and sensual space that physically involves the viewer."[12] Lee sometimes applies his painted streak

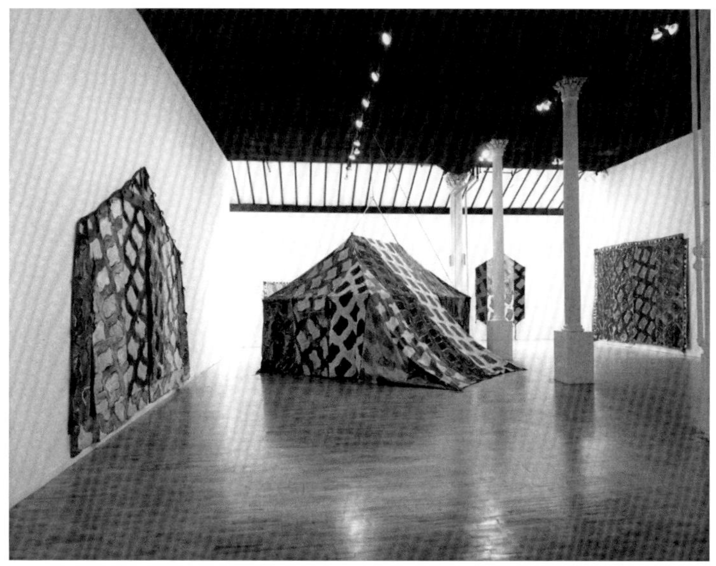

fig. 5
Claude Viallat
installation view: *Claude Viallat*,
142 GREENE, Leo Castelli Gallery, 1982

directly to the wall or even on the floor. But even if for him the painting hanging on the wall is the general rule and his quest consists of trying to unify the painting with the exhibition space, "It is the entire space that becomes the painting."[13] Hence his desire to create a relationship, an encounter, between the interior and the exterior, the painted and the unpainted, is the foundation of his quest. As for the sculptures, the dialogue between industrial and natural materials in Lee's work has very little to do with Viallat's fragile and precarious assemblages using ropes, driftwood, and recovered materials. However, Lee observes in Viallat's paintings, and more generally in the approaches of some Supports/Surfaces members, a work of *deconstruction*, which is not limited to the internal needs of the painting. It is also significant that the two artists use this same term and place it at the heart of their work.

> Lee Ufan: *"The Supports/Surfaces artists have clearly shown that the work of art is not defined solely within the painted surface. They questioned how we exhibit. How do we install works in space? Outside? Inside? Hung on the wall? Hung or hooked with a string? These works existed precisely due to the links between the exterior and their internal elements, and also through reflecting on the conditions of exhibition. It was therefore not the internal elements that were the focus, but always the link with the exterior that the Supports/Surfaces artists were looking for."*

> Claude Viallat: *"But always in accordance with the space, the reality of the space. For me, it would be unthinkable to solidify the works. They are a bit like tools for creating the exhibition, in other words, each time they must be arranged in relation to each other, and this relation is more important than the solidified image of the object."*

We should also mention the "group" (which is not a single group, but rather an ex-post-facto grouping) of Korean painters who were later assembled under the term Dansaekhwa, which can be translated as "Monochrome." Lee, although living in Japan, had a great impact on this movement of abstract painters in his native country with which he is often associated. In a way, he was the theoretician, and through the method of formal repetition (Park Seo-Bo), physical action, for example, pushing the pictorial material from the back of the canvas (Ha Chong-Hyun), manipulation of materials, and work in and with the surface, we see similarities with Viallat's approaches to painting and in general with the pictorial principles disseminated by Supports/Surfaces. This is especially true since, unlike Mono-ha, which is essentially a reflection on the use of materials and on sculpture, and like Supports/Surfaces, Dansaekhwa raises the question of surface treatment and painting, although with very different means.

> Lee Ufan: *"At the time (early 1970s), South Korea was under a military government, and any possibility of expression was very limited, very constrained. To dodge censorship, Korean artists actually did things that didn't make much sense: for example, printing the same motif with ink, layering it. That's how we really got around all kinds of limitations. The situation did not allow Korean artists to envisage a new form of expression, but really forced them to think before doing*

anything. What are the surfaces? What are the supports? And what is the role of ink, paint, tools? How can we articulate these different elements? That is how they created their works. So from that point of view, there are a lot of similarities between Dansaekhwa and Supports/Surfaces. And I can confirm that it was a really influential movement at the time in Korea."

The two artists have remained faithful to the main principles that guided their works beginning in the 1970s. Viallat was able to state, "I don't see my work as progressing over time, linearly. It moves in a spiral from a core."[14] If the formula does not strictly apply to Lee, the fact remains that a continuity in coherence based on the principle of "themes and variations" govern the paths of these two artists. No denial, no backtracking comes into play in the development of their work. While Viallat can state that today he can create a painting that repeats an earlier painting,[15] Lee has returned to the *Relatum* of 1968 (initially titled *Phenomenon and Perception B*) in recent exhibitions without it being exactly the same sculpture, as the materials and contexts are not identical. Undoubtedly, we could speak of a common ethos seen in two artists from the same generation, confronted in their early years with similar reflections on the evolution of the art of their time and determined to reinvent its foundations.

Unless otherwise stated, quotes from Lee Ufan and Claude Viallat are taken from an interview with the author dated October 20, 2022.

1 Though they had been invited to the exhibition, the Supports/Surfaces group was only represented by the wall inscription "Supports/Surfaces: Peinture Cahiers théoriques" followed by the names A-P. Arnal, V. Bioulès, L. Cane, M. Devade, D. Dezeuze, J-P. Pincemin. Only Claude Viallat and Noël Dolla exhibited works.

2 Included in the exhibition were Enokura Koji, Koshimizu Susumu, and Yoshida Katsuro.

3 Narita Katsuhiko, Sekine Nobuo, Takamatsu Jiro, and Tanaka Shintaro were grouped together by the critic Tono Yoshiaki under the name 4 Bossots.

4 *Tel Quel* was a literary magazine founded in 1960. The main members of the magazine at the time of Supports/Surfaces were Philippe Sollers, its founder, as well as Marcelin Pleynet, Julia Kristeva, and Roland Barthes.

5 *Supports/Surfaces: A Moment, A Movement* (Saint-Étienne: Ceysson Éditions d'art, 2010; English translation 2015).

6 Nikolaï Tarabukin (1889–1956) was an art historian, specializing in Russian Constructivism.

7 André Leroi-Gourhan (1911–1986) was an archaeologist and paleontologist, leading prehistorian, and author of the masterwork *La Préhistoire de l'art occidental (The Art of Prehistoric Man in Western Europe).*

8 Lee Ufan, *Un art de la rencontre (The Search for Encounter)* (Arles: Actes Sud, 2019), 89.

9 *Phase–Mother Earth 1968*, Kobe Suma Rikyu Park Contemporary Sculpture Exhibition, October 1968.

10 Bijutsu Techō, February 1970, reproduced in English in *Requiem for the Sun: The Art of Mono-ha* (Los Angeles: Blum & Poe, 2012).

11 Lee Ufan refers here to Narita Katsuhiko.

12 Claude Viallat, interview with Alfred Pacquement for *Claude Viallat: Les années 1980 (Claude Viallat: the 1980s)*, Galerie Daniel Templon, Paris, June – July 2016.

13 "Alfred Pacquement in conversation with Lee Ufan," *Lee Ufan: From Line, From Point, From Wind*, Pace London, September – October 2015.

14 Interview with Claude Viallat in exhibition catalog *Claude Viallat* (Saint-Étienne: Musée d'art et d'industrie, 1974), 11.

15 Ibid.

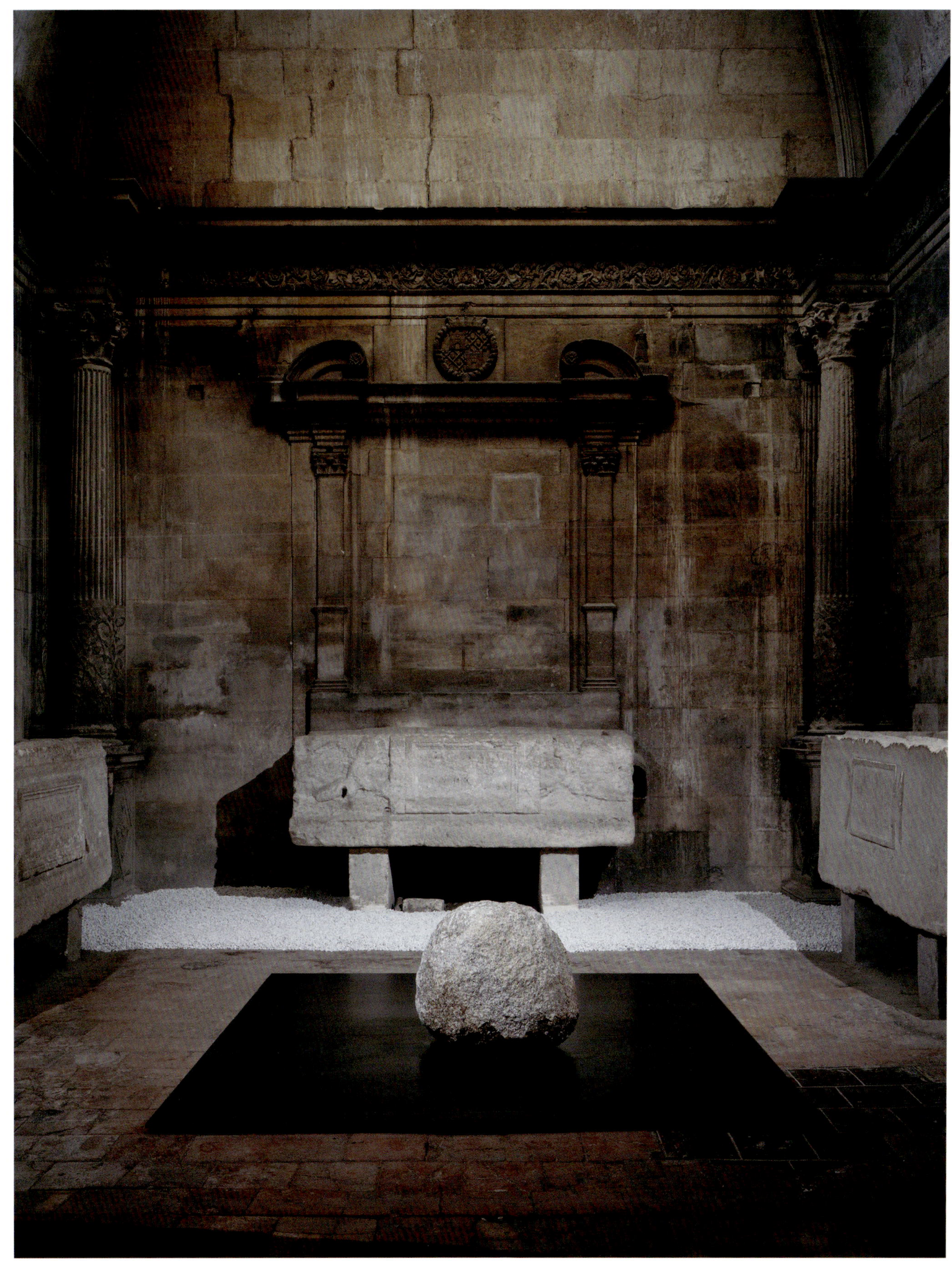

fig. 6
Lee Ufan
installation view:
Alyscamps, Arles, 2022

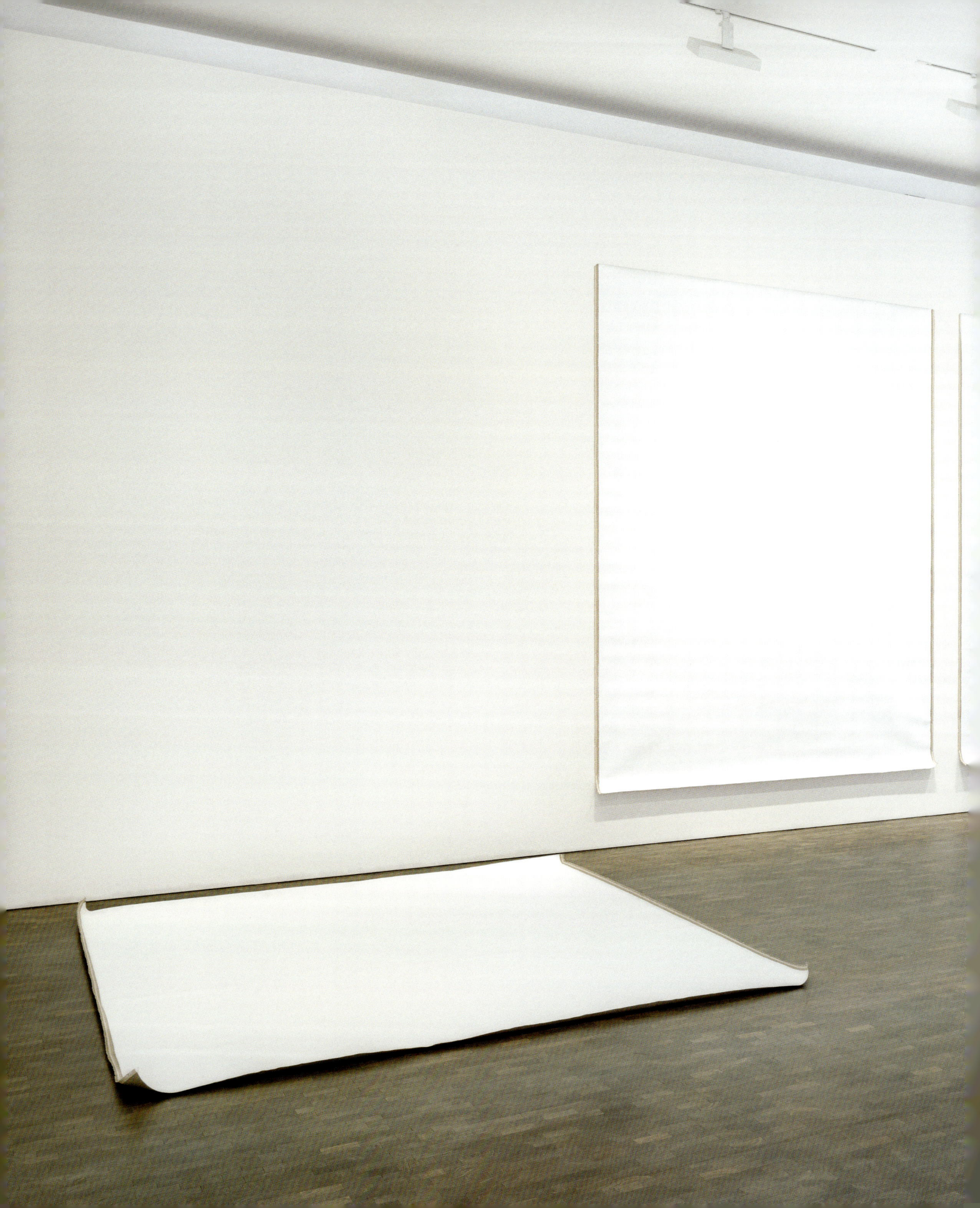

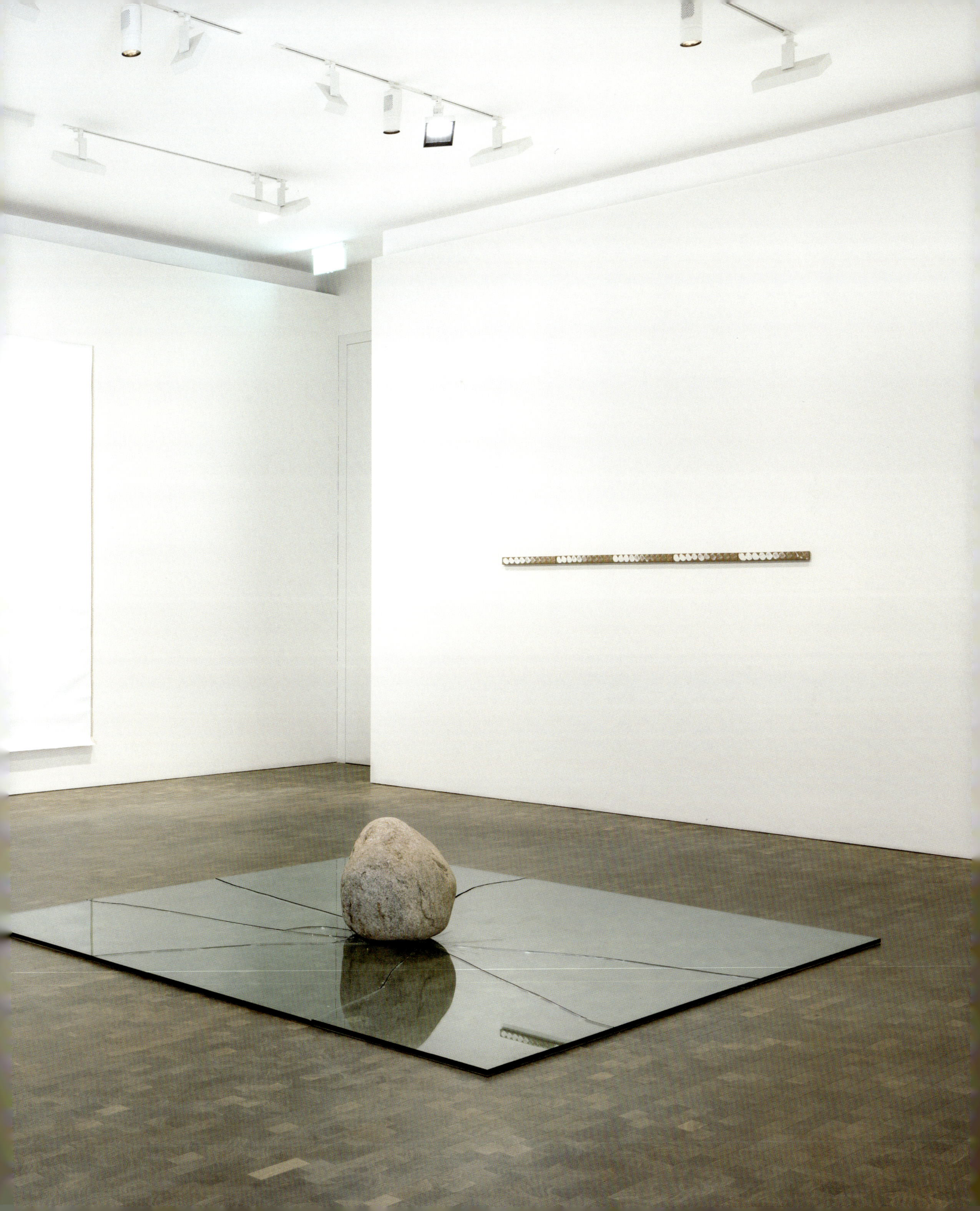

Lee Ufan

RELATUM

1968/2023

glass and stone
glass 110 ¼ × 98 7/16 × 13/16" | 280 × 250 × 2.1 cm
stone 23 ⅝ × 15 ¾ × 15 ¾" | 60 × 40 × 40 cm

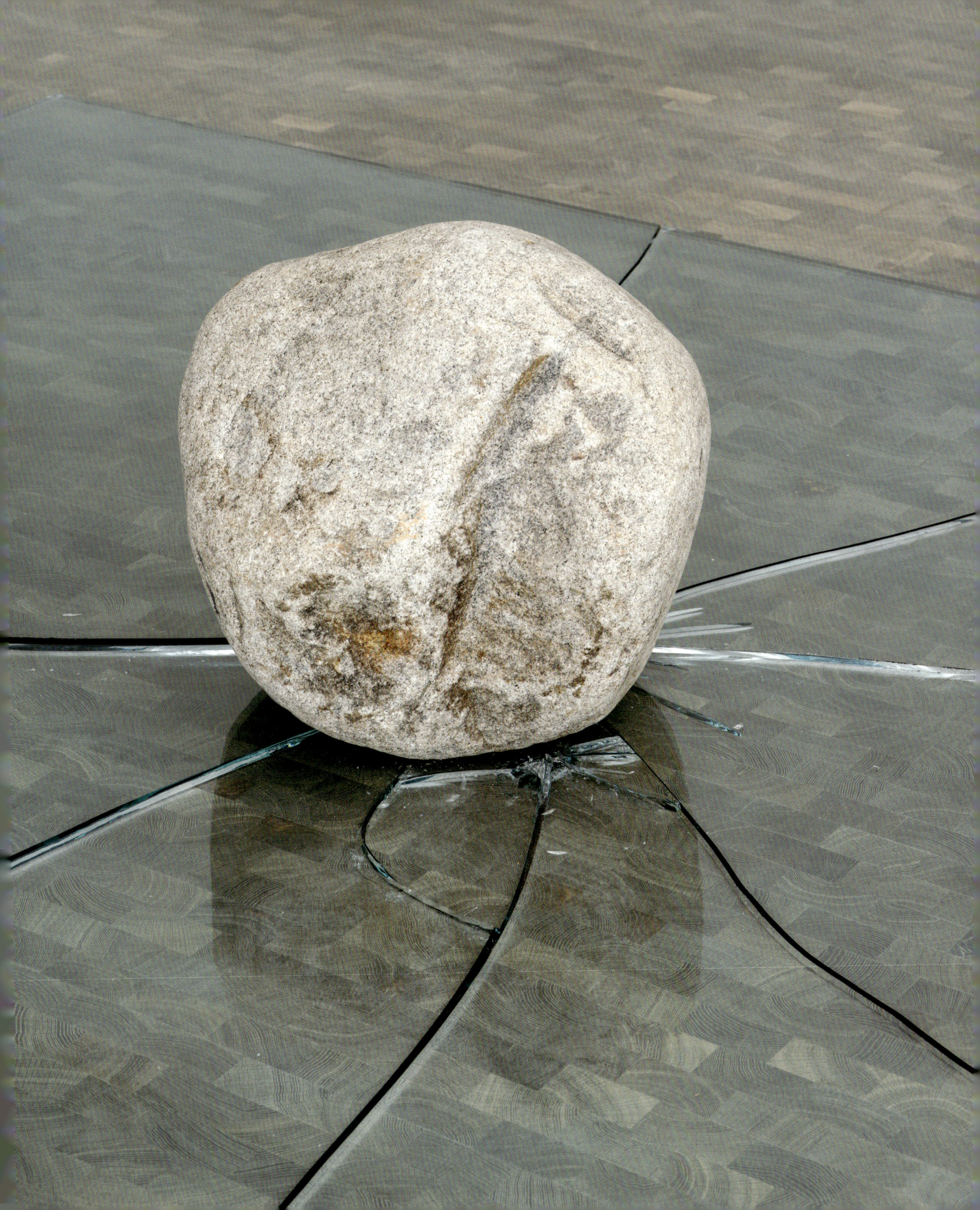

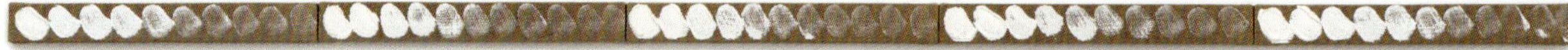

Lee Ufan

FROM POINT

1977

acrylic on canvas
5 canvases, each 1 15⁄16 × 15 ¾" | 5 × 40 x 3 cm
overall 1 15⁄16 × 79 ¼ × 1 3⁄16" | 5 × 201.3 × 3 cm

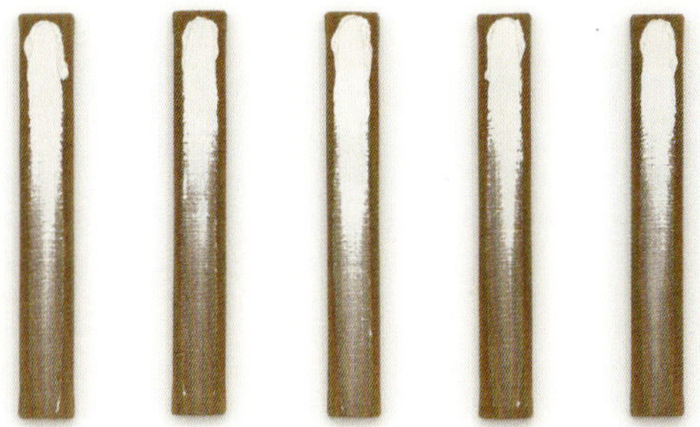

Lee Ufan

FROM LINE

1977

acrylic on canvas
5 canvases, each 15 ¾ × 1 15⁄16" | 40 × 4.9 x 3 cm
overall 15 ¾ × 25 9⁄16 × 1 3⁄16" | 40 × 65 × 3 cm

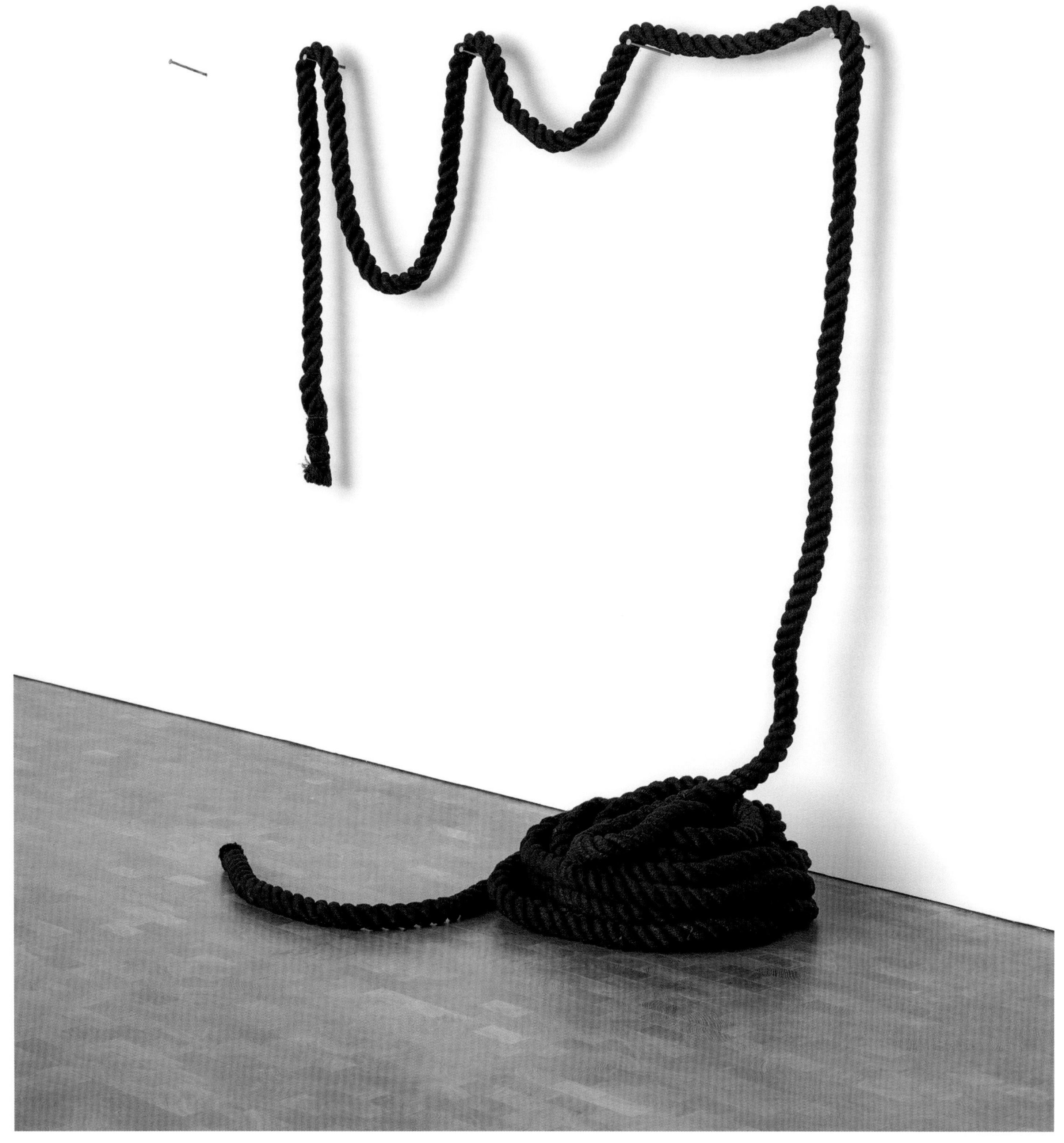

Lee Ufan

RELATUM — THE ROPE DRAIN

1974/2023

rope and nails
dimensions variable

RELATUM

1977/2023

cotton and wire
dimensions variable

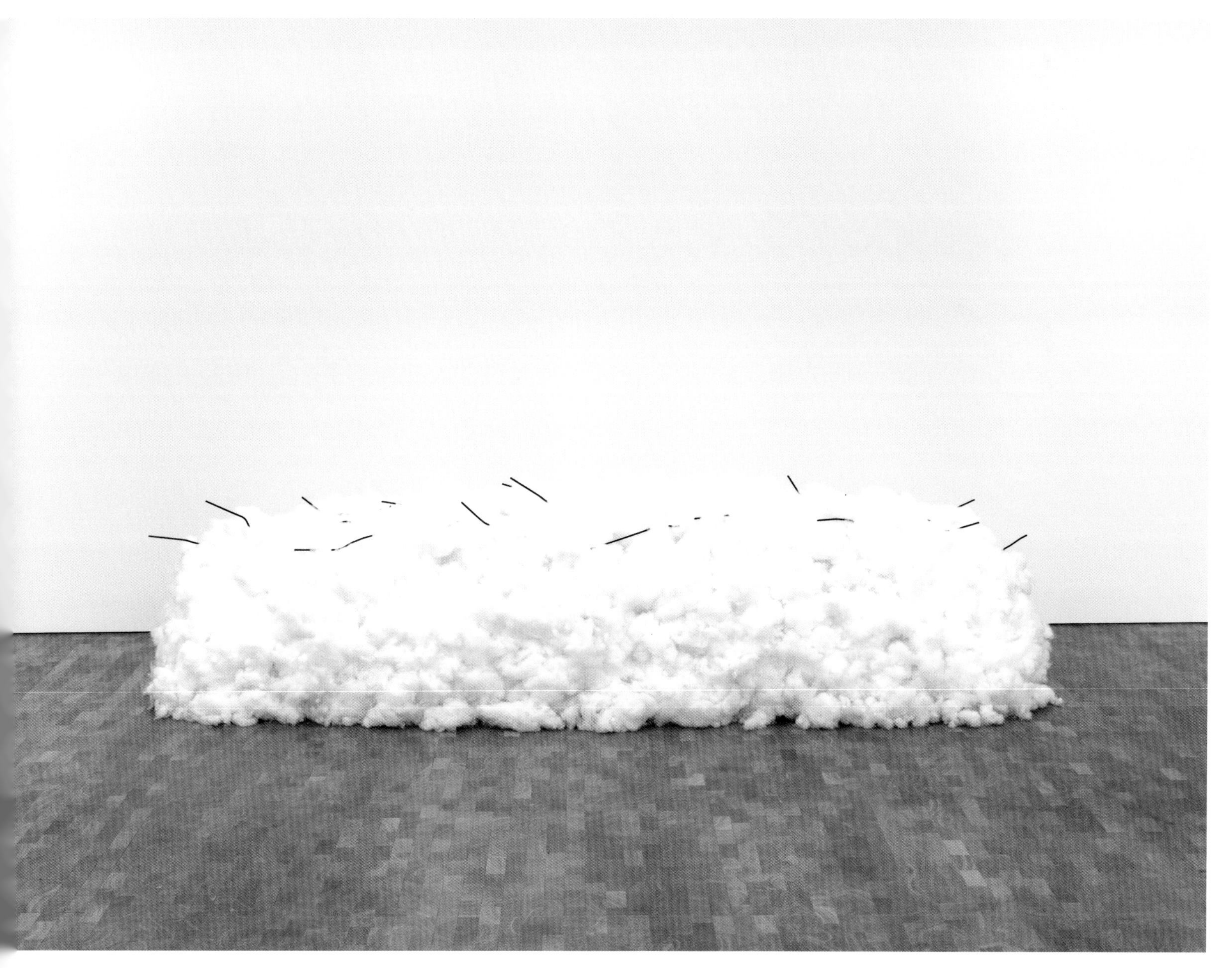

Lee Ufan | **RELATUM — THINGS AND WORDS**
1969/2023
canvas
3 canvases, each 118 ⅛ × 78 ¾" | 300 × 200 cm

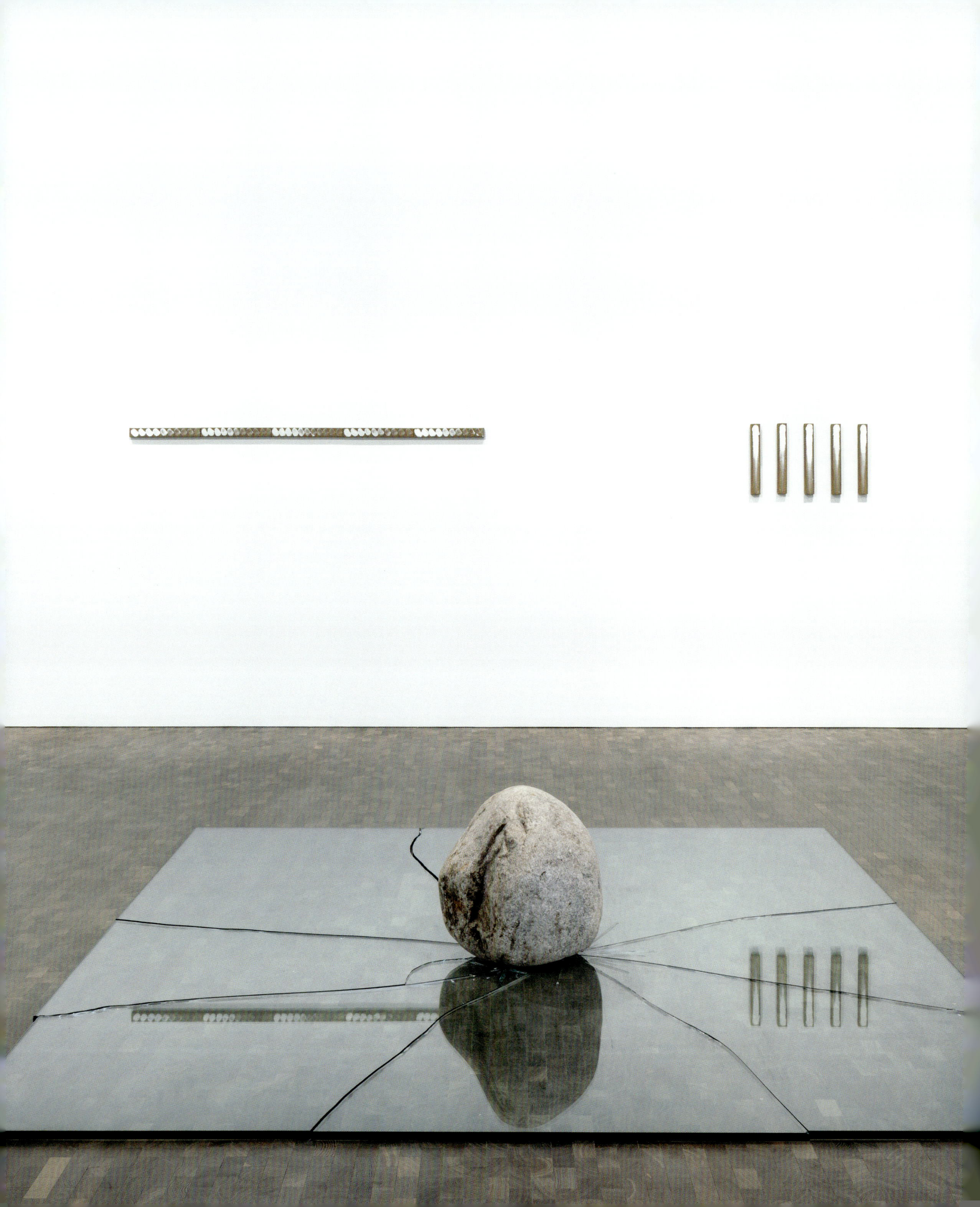

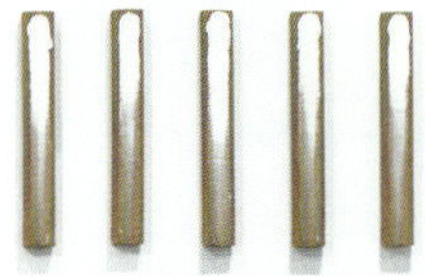

Lee Ufan

SUPPORTS/SURFACES: ON THE BEGINNING OF EXPRESSION

In retrospect, the modern period was a unique era of imperialism, characterized by the expansion and proliferation of the ego. Colonialism smothered the world with its own concept of the self, as is evident even in abstract art. No historical period has turned its back on nature, mythology, and social problems like the modern age, while still striving for the autonomous and abstract development of human symbols. The all-over style and the all-encompassing power of the surface plane are emblematic of modern art. In other words, you can see that such expression is expression of the self; externality and alterity are therefore ignored or excluded. However, this trend came to an end with the collapse of imperialism after World War II. Subsequently, as capitalism matured and socialism became meaningless, there was no choice but to dismantle the anthropocentric ideology. And artists, though bewildered and confused, embarked on unprecedented experiments with painting and the act of creating.

The common thread in these new experiments in Europe, the United States, and East Asia is the retreat of the subject and the acceptance of the external and alterity. In other words, expression freed itself from the ego and became fluid. The methods and appearance of this expression differ depending on the historical and regional context. Nevertheless, the focus on mediating action, the existence of the support and the qualities of the material freed from the constraints of symbols, led expression toward the unknown. From the late 1960s to the early 1970s, the art world in Europe, the United States, and East Asia was in a state of upheaval in terms of the starting point of expression. That such fundamental experiments spread almost simultaneously around the world, transcending the borders of different regions and cultures, represented a surprising, unprecedented, and wonderful moment in the history of art.

Trends such as Arte Povera in Italy, environmental art in England and the United States, Anti-form in the United States, the Supports/Surfaces group in France, Mono-ha in Japan, and, a little later, Dansaekhwa monochrome painting in South Korea were all impacted in different ways by historical circumstances and geopolitics. However, viewed macroscopically, these phenomena appear very similar. In the Art Informel and Action painting movements that preceded them, drawing and the act of creating represented the final stage of modern aesthetic thought. Nouveau Réalisme also falls into this category. All these movements were set on an axis of presupposed expression. Thus, the expansive tendencies that followed can be understood as movements that encouraged unpresupposed expression.

Arte Povera, Anti-form, and Mono-ha focused on the raw state of materials before expression and the relationship between materials and people, while environmental art, Anti-form, and, in some cases, Mono-ha engaged with the exterior world and invited in the things and spaces found there. In contrast, Supports/Surfaces and Dansaekhwa were composed of many artists with a strong interest in painting, and, as the name Supports/Surfaces implies, the spatial and chromatic composition of the support and the painted object were an important characteristic of the movement. In Dansaekhwa, the organic relationship between the support and the action itself became the expression. In all these cases, expression was no longer the development of a strong self-image, as it had been before. Unlike the destruction of the subject seen in Dada or Surrealist images, the emphasis on the support itself and the use of anonymity and contingency led to the formation of neutral expressions. Thus, the subject and the image are limited, and a new world of expression opens up, mixing the acceptance of the external that remains uncontrolled, the proliferation of organic symbols, the transformation of the material, and the intervention of action.

My first encounter with Supports/Surfaces took place in the summer of 1971 at the Bois de Vincennes, where the Biennale de Paris was being held. I was a participant and had a problem with one of the artists in the group. A thin rope with many pieces of white fabric hanging from it straddled the space just above my artwork, and I was arguing to have it removed. This led to a confrontation with Daniel Abadie, Georges Boudaille's assistant, who was the general director of the Biennale. (He then became director of the Jeu de Paume and organized one of my exhibitions. Another assistant was Alfred Pacquement, who always supported me.) Supports/Surfaces occupied a large corner of the gallery, and the artists had spread their works throughout various other spaces. As was the case with Mono-ha in Japan, their works were quite bold and reflected a sort of obstinacy no matter where they were located. Despite this mishap, I felt an immediate affinity with their work. Claude Viallat, whom I met at that time, became a lifelong friend. Later, he recommended mounting a Mono-ha exhibition at the modern art museum in Saint-Étienne, and I organized his solo exhibition at the Kamakura Gallery in Tokyo. I got close to Toni Grand, since we were represented by the same gallery in Paris, and in 1977 I invited him to stay with me in Tokyo and helped him get a solo exhibition at Komai Gallery. I also met Mark Devade by chance, and I visited his studio. He was studying Chinese then, and we sometimes enjoyed writing sinograms together in a café in Paris.

Supports/Surfaces was a group of artists living mostly in the south of France, with the exception of a few who were in Paris. Unlike the more conceptual artists whose work was based on clear ideas, such as Daniel Buren, Olivier Mosset, Michel Parmentier, and Niele Toroni, Supports/Surfaces was a group whose work appeared to be somewhat unstable. In this regard, their work made me feel a novel sense of risk-taking and dynamism that did not easily indicate the direction it would take. The nature of this fluid and incomplete expression seemed appropriate for an era that served as an interlude between deconstruction and construction.

Early Supports/Surfaces paintings did not employ readymade canvases but used a variety of irregularly shaped fabrics. Many of them were dyed or painted with colors or shapes. Viallat paints an endless proliferation of distinctive amoebic shapes and colors on fabrics or tents with or without patterns. Louis Cane combines strips of dyed fabric in a square frame around a hollow center with long pieces of fabric that spill over the frame. Jean-Pierre Pincemin creates patchworks of white fabric that he methodically folds; he dyes the folds and then partially removes the color. Noël Dolla suspends fabrics of different colors and motifs in the air or on the wall. The colors and motifs applied to the fabric are presented as disturbing phenomena, like an unexpected event, something that subtly deviates from the conventional system of a painting.

Grand used tree branches to scrape off part of the surface and either segment them into multiple sections or gather them into irregular shapes. Bernard Pagès and other artists created sculptures that combine tree branches and concrete blocks, simple wooden beams with colored materials, natural stones with industrial waste, or a large steel mesh cube filled with a pile of gravel almost overflowing the mesh. Here, the artist's intervention is in tune with the existence and character of the materials, and the combination and rearrangement of natural and industrial materials represent its expression. They could be characterized as events that activate the external nature of materials through the intervention of the artists. Each piece has its own personality, but in one way or another I feel they have an affinity with the works of Arte Povera, Anti-form, and Mono-ha, as well as environmental artists such as Robert Smithson. This is why the works of Mono-ha somewhat resemble the works of Arte Povera that preceded them. It is proof that similar approaches occurred simultaneously around the world, even without an exchange of information, and you could describe these works as examples of the relationship between circumstances and imagination.

The artists' interpretation of the material supporting expression we see in Supports/Surfaces is exceptional. In Abstract Expressionism, action prevailed over fabric and color, and in Arte Povera and Mono-ha, the material itself is often left in a raw state. In contrast, Supports/Surfaces combines the artist's concept and actions with the existence of and reliance on the material. The material is not an element to create symbols; it emphasizes the quality of anonymous signs and neutral actions. This was notably the case with Viallat, Cane, Pincemin, André-Pierre Arnal, Grand. They did not treat the material as sacred or transform it into something else through concepts or actions. Mark Devade is a well-known theorist, and his theory of color ("D'une peinture chromatique," *Tel Quel*, April 1970, p. 41) highlights the nature of the group. He sees color as a fluid material existence that is linked to visual culture, and he believes painting is realized in the imagination through the intersection of colors and supports. Admittedly, many expressions looked like this in the early days of the group. However, in reality, it seems that the power of pictorial composition had gradually taken precedence over the phenomenological character of color as an external element. Similar changes can be found in other movements. Painting forms a pictorial world, and sculpture forms a sculptural world, no matter what path is taken. This is why the expressions of painting and sculpture seem to be a fundamental and unavoidable requirement within the framework of vision.

The influence of Simon Hantaï and Martin Barré is also seen in the choice of fabrics, the stamp technique, and the use of signs and empty spaces. Nevertheless, compared to the works of Hantaï and other artists who are deeply rooted in the plasticity of painting, Supports/Surfaces shows a deep awareness of how expression manifests itself in relation to the external world, and that is why its expressions are full of an immaterial possibility that cannot be contained by the painting. It gives the impression of experiencing a new form of expression. The construction of a modern, hermetic space of consciousness that uses material as building blocks for the manifestation of symbols has collapsed. Today there is a demand for expression that recognizes the external nature of materials and comes to life with the autonomy of actions liberated from the ego. In this sense, you could say that this movement of artists who sought to generate expression from the relationship between support and surface was the embodiment of the era.

To put it another way, Supports/Surfaces was a movement that questioned how to achieve expression. This must be why the relationship between the support and the surface became the name of their movement. This framework seems to have been an appropriate point of view to question the origin of expression. And yet, while it offered the movement an opportunity to progress, it struggled to serve as a driving force for its continuation and development. Thus, this classification is very likely to lead to the deterioration of various expressions. In the future, there will probably be many debates about what is support and what is surface, and whether to ignore them. Such discussions would surely be even more intense if we still had passionate discussion forums like *Tel Quel*, which was so emblematic of the French love of debate. As far as I know, the group disbanded in the early 1970s, as did Mono-ha. Since then, the artists have each followed their own paths. Perhaps partly because of the strong tradition of painting and sculpture in France, many of these artists moved deeper and deeper with their work, with some of them moving toward softer expressions.

In any event, when we think about what the 1970s were in terms of expression, the presence and importance of the Supports/Surfaces artists is essential. They did not frame the problem in terms of presenting an idea but argued that there was something inherent in the original conditions, a genuinely French attitude. In *The Order of Things*, Michel Foucault describes how the envelopment of things in words led to a rupture that made today's world difficult to understand. Indeed, the 1970s were a period of inquiry when the relationship between things and words was examined, and there were many movements toward new forms of expression. Since we humans are part of the progression of history, we cannot start from zero. However, considering the shattered view of modernity centered on symbols, Supports/Surfaces, which seriously tried to address the external nature of things, remains relevant. I would like to create an opportunity to reexamine their work and bring them back into the spotlight.

August 25, 2022

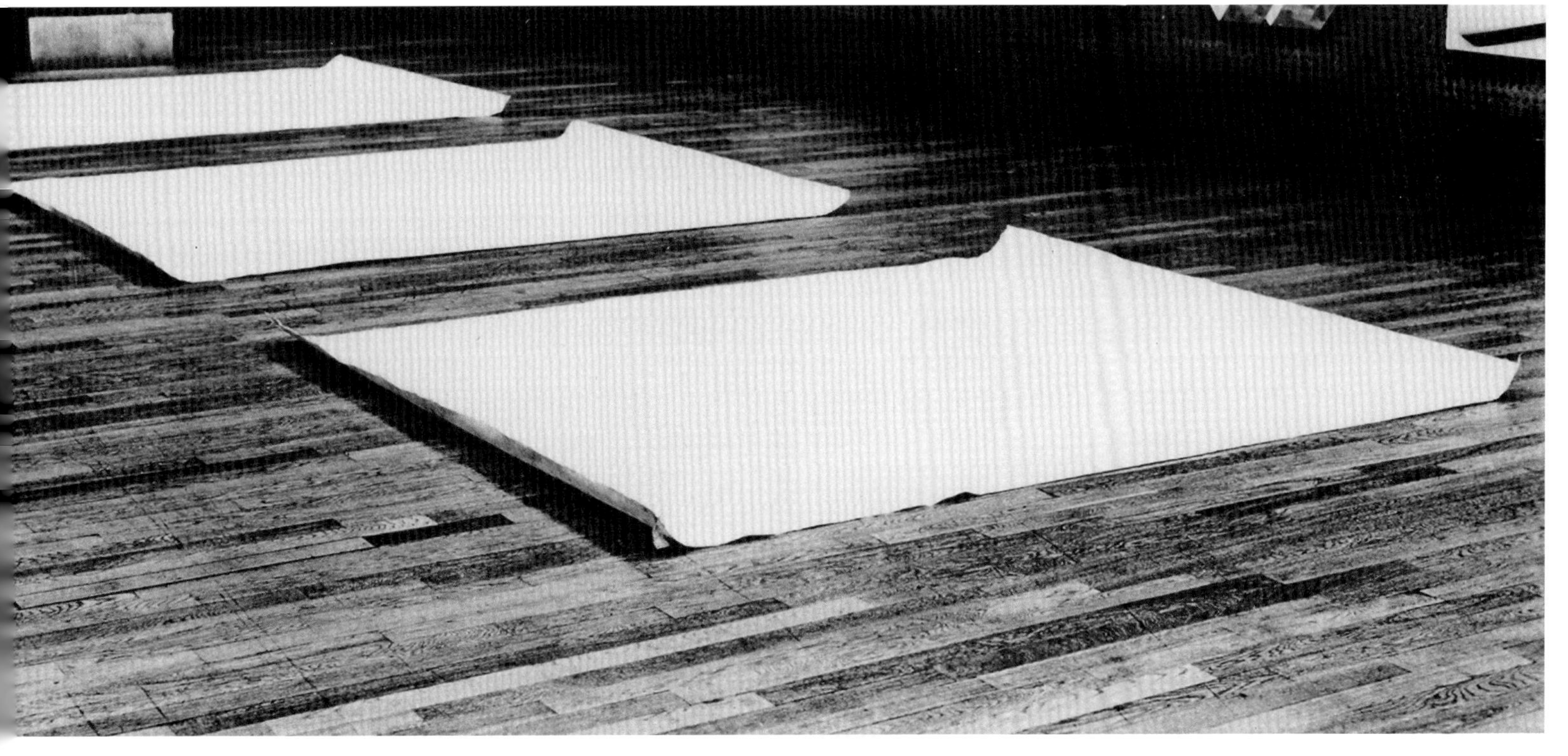

Lee Ufan
Things and Words, 1969
paper and glue
3 sheets, approximately 236 ¼ × 78 ¾" | 600 × 200 cm overall
installation view: 9th Contemporary Art Exhibition
of Japan, Tokyo Metropolitan Art Museum,
May 10–30, 1969

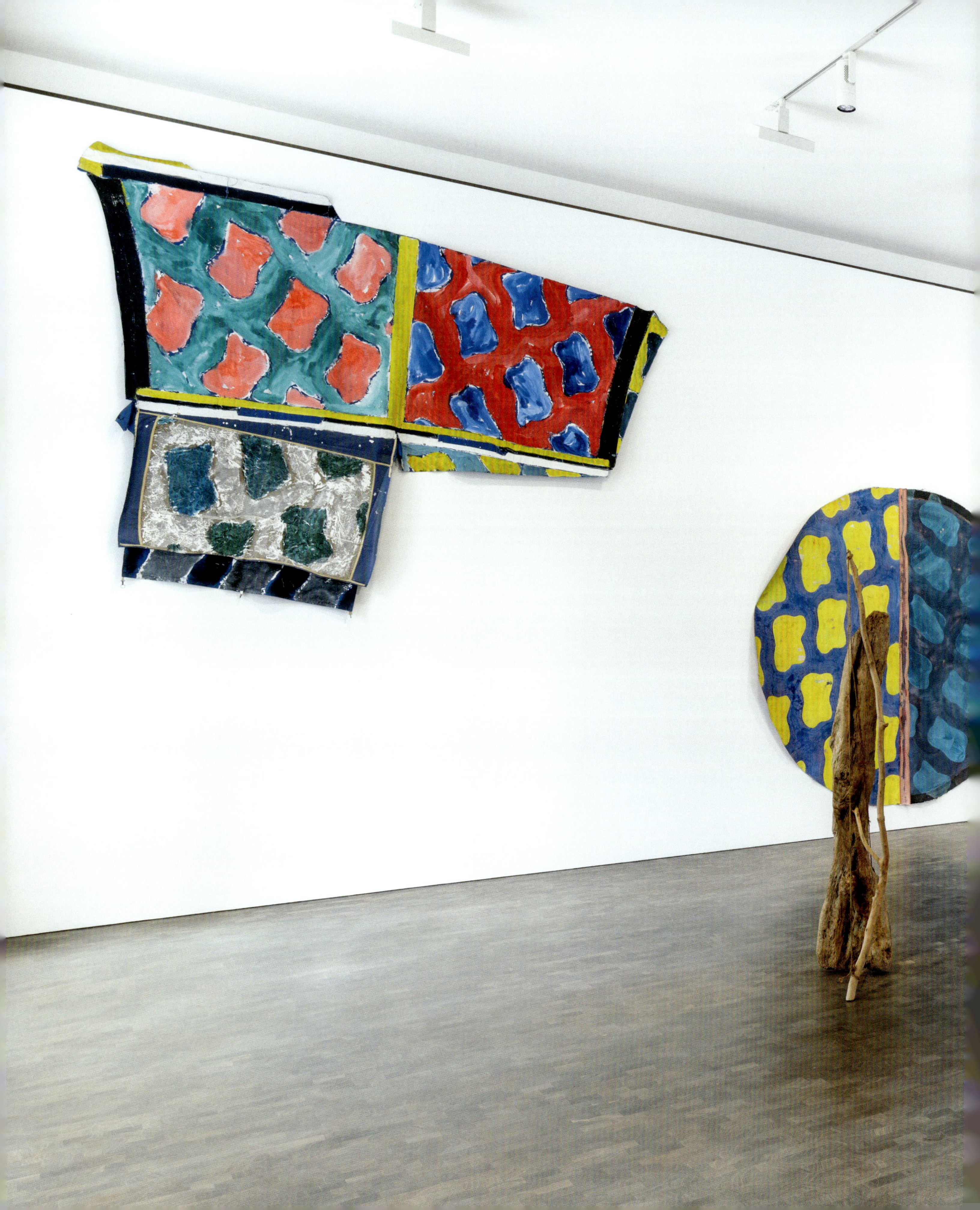

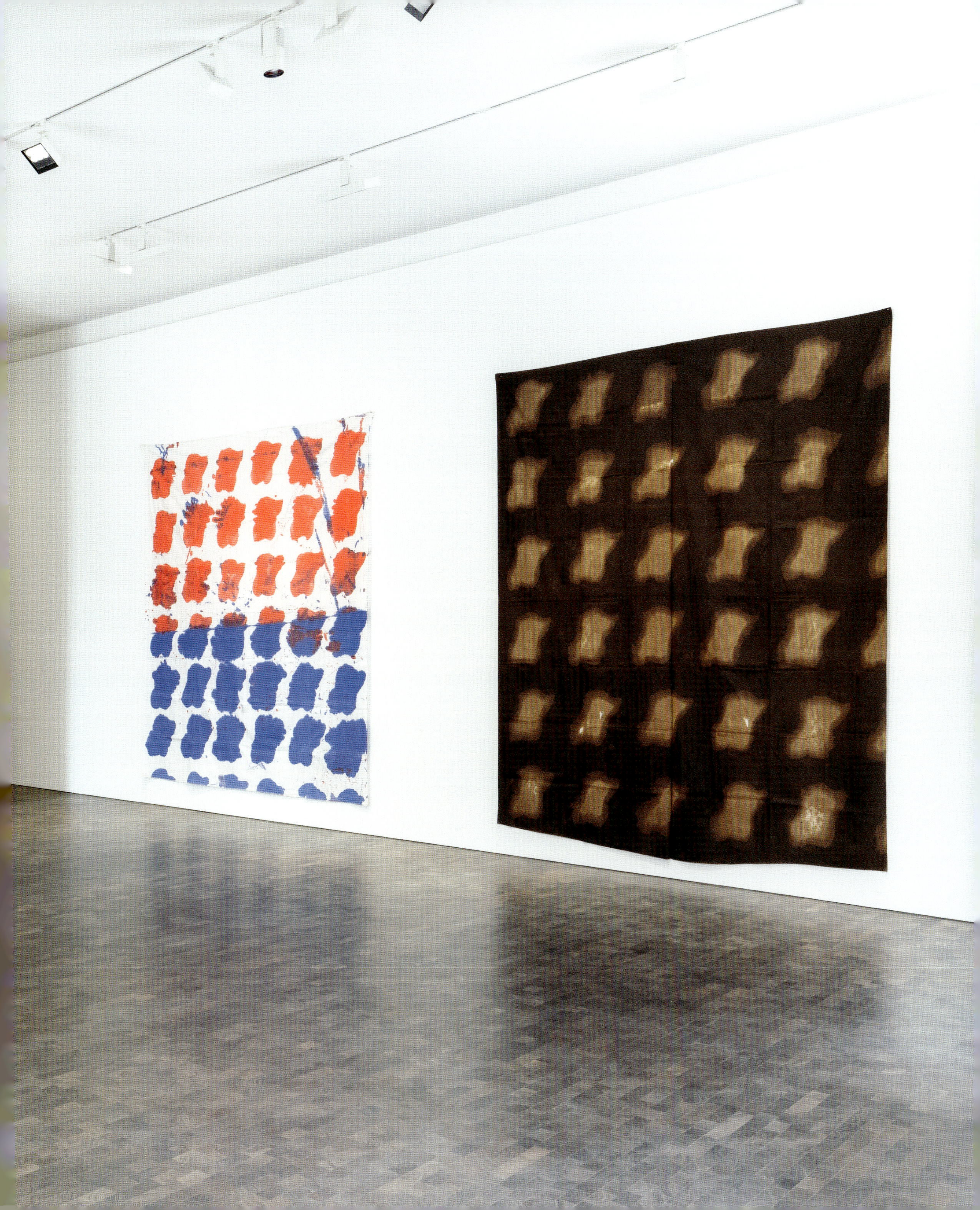

Claude Viallat

1975/028

1975

mordant dye on canvas
98 ⅜ × 78 ¾" | 249.9 × 200 cm

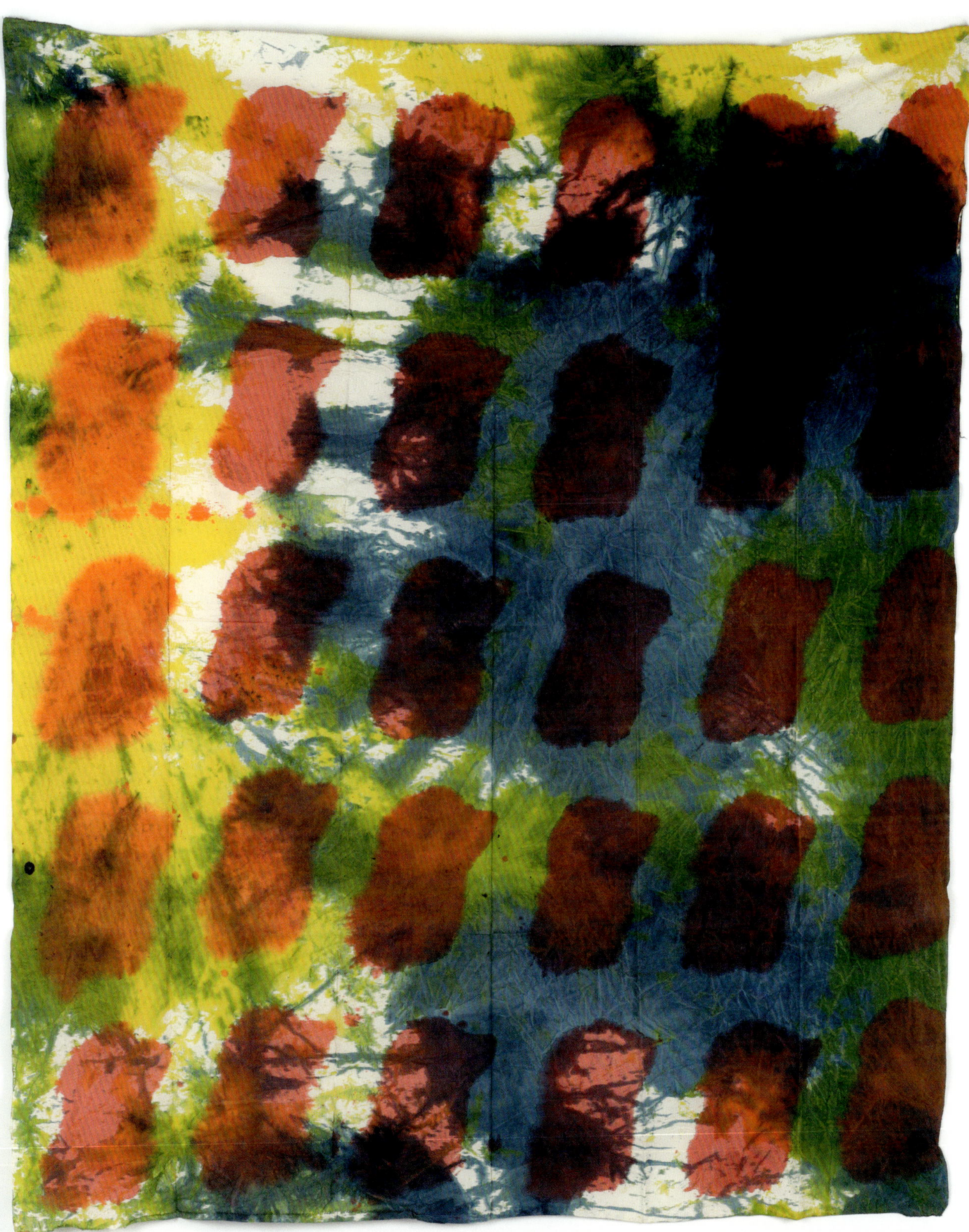

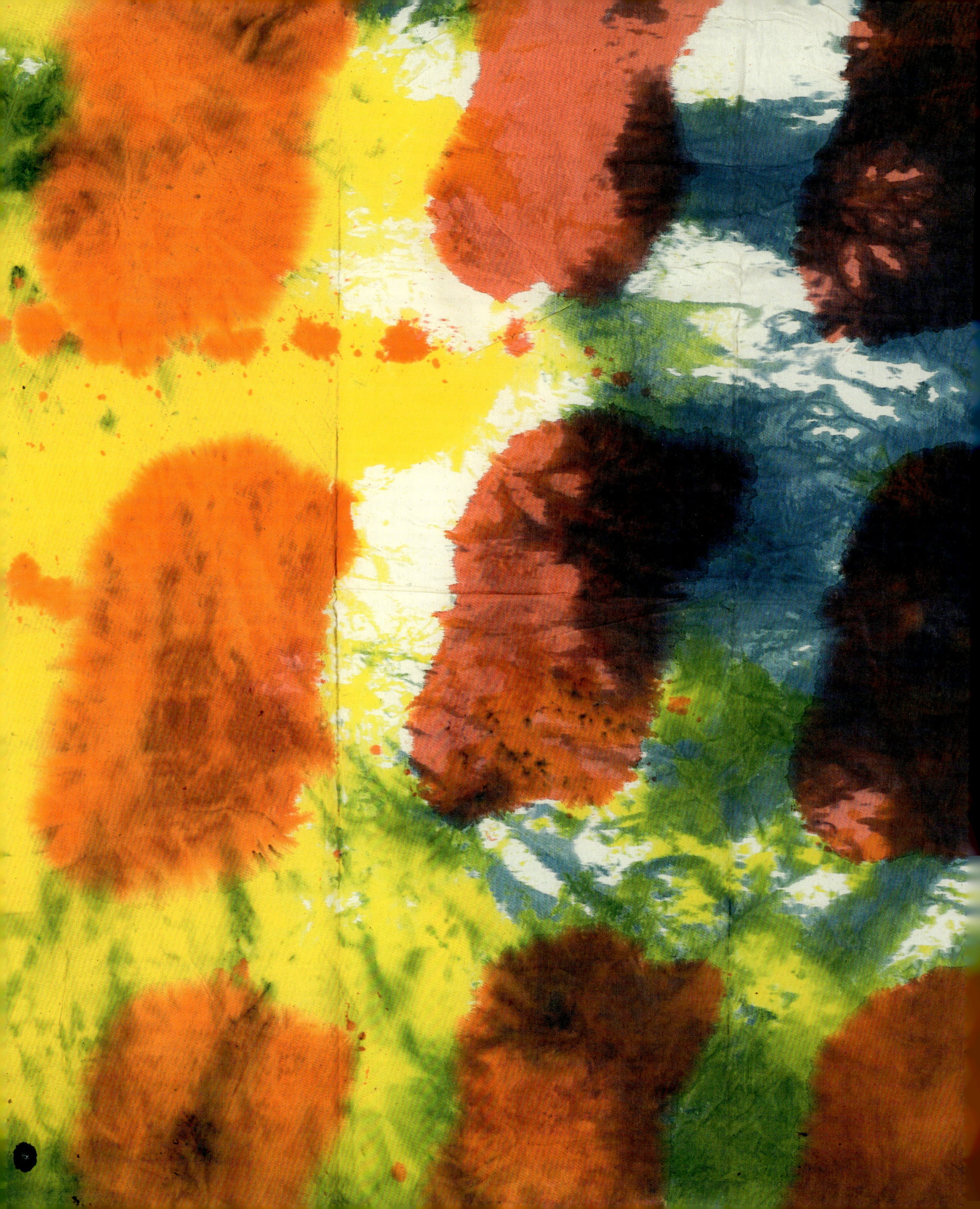

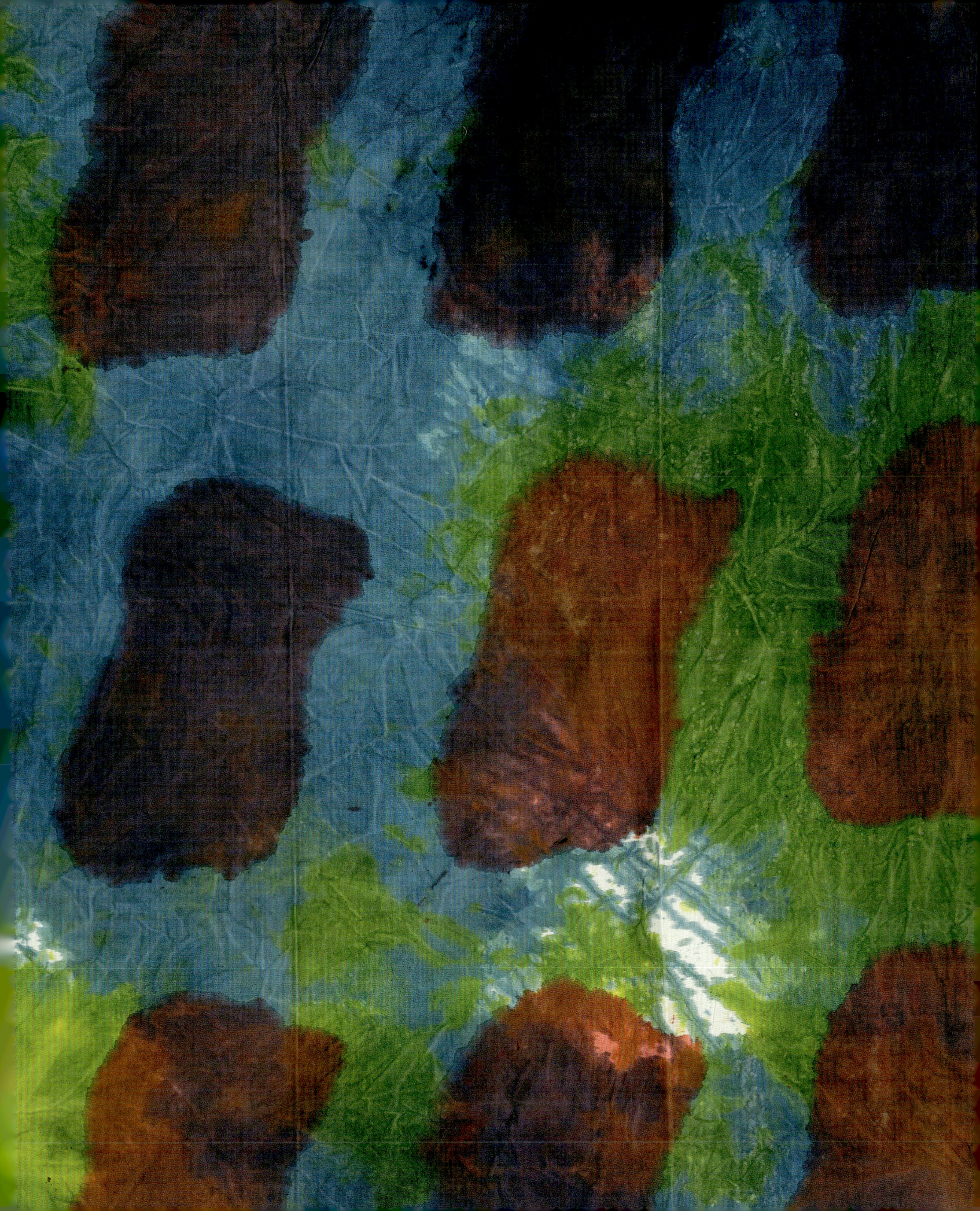

Claude Viallat

1973/003

1973

carbonyl on fabric
117 5⁄16 × 83 ½" | 298 × 212.1 cm

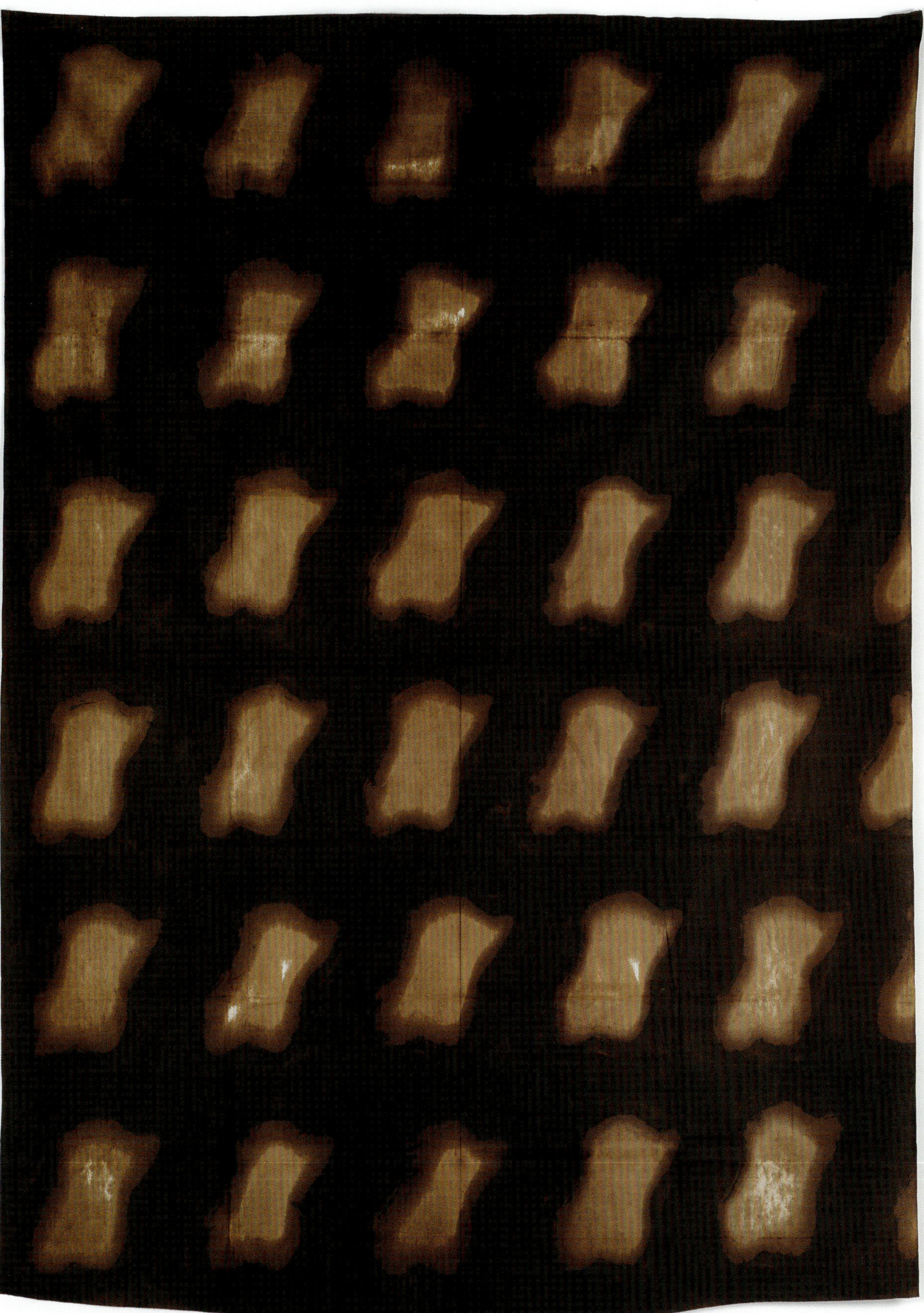

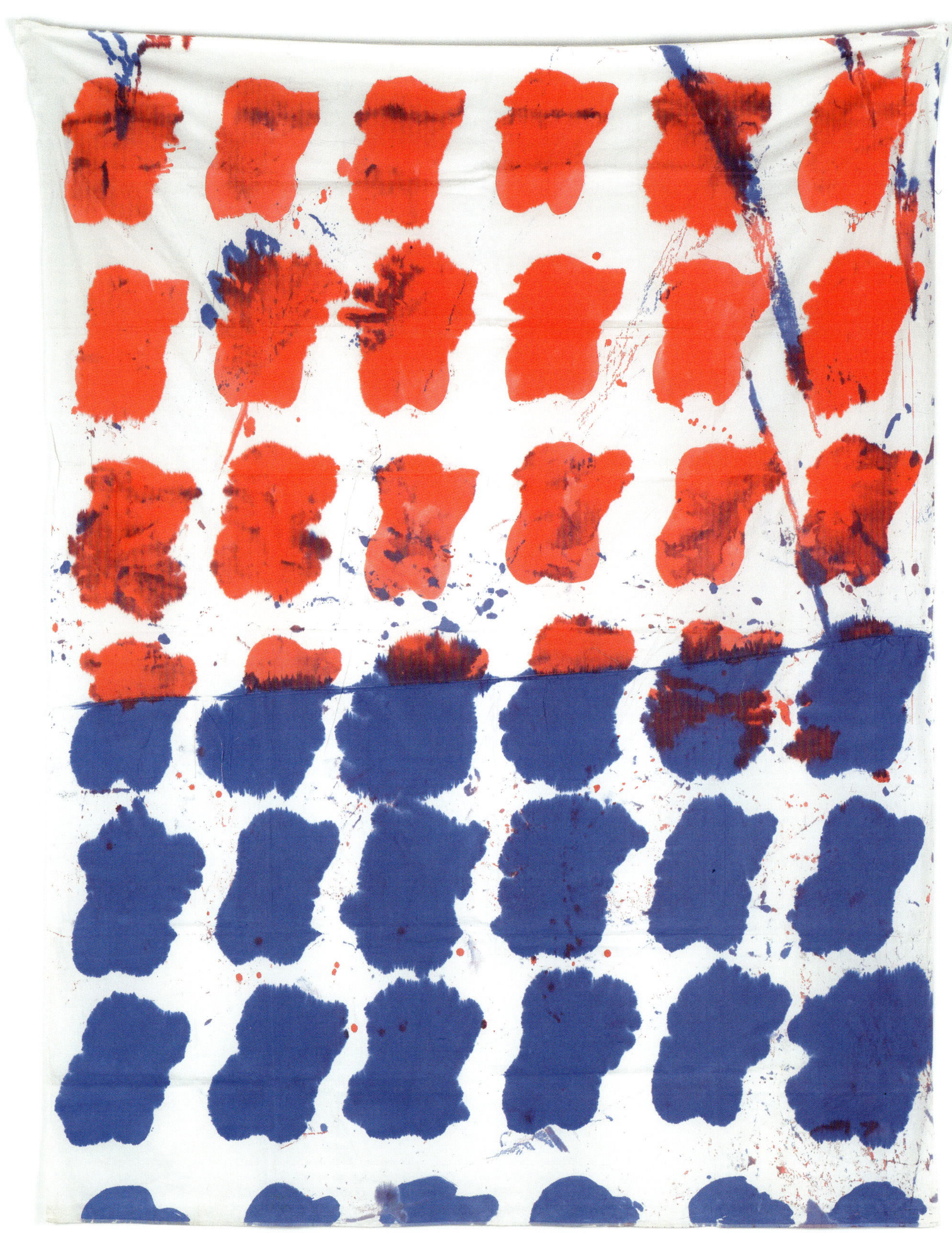

Claude Viallat

1975/016

1975

acrylic on 2 canvases stitched together
110 ¼ × 82 ¹¹⁄₁₆" | 280 × 210 cm

Claude Viallat

1977/054

1977

acrylic on circular canvas
diameter 92 ½" | 235 cm

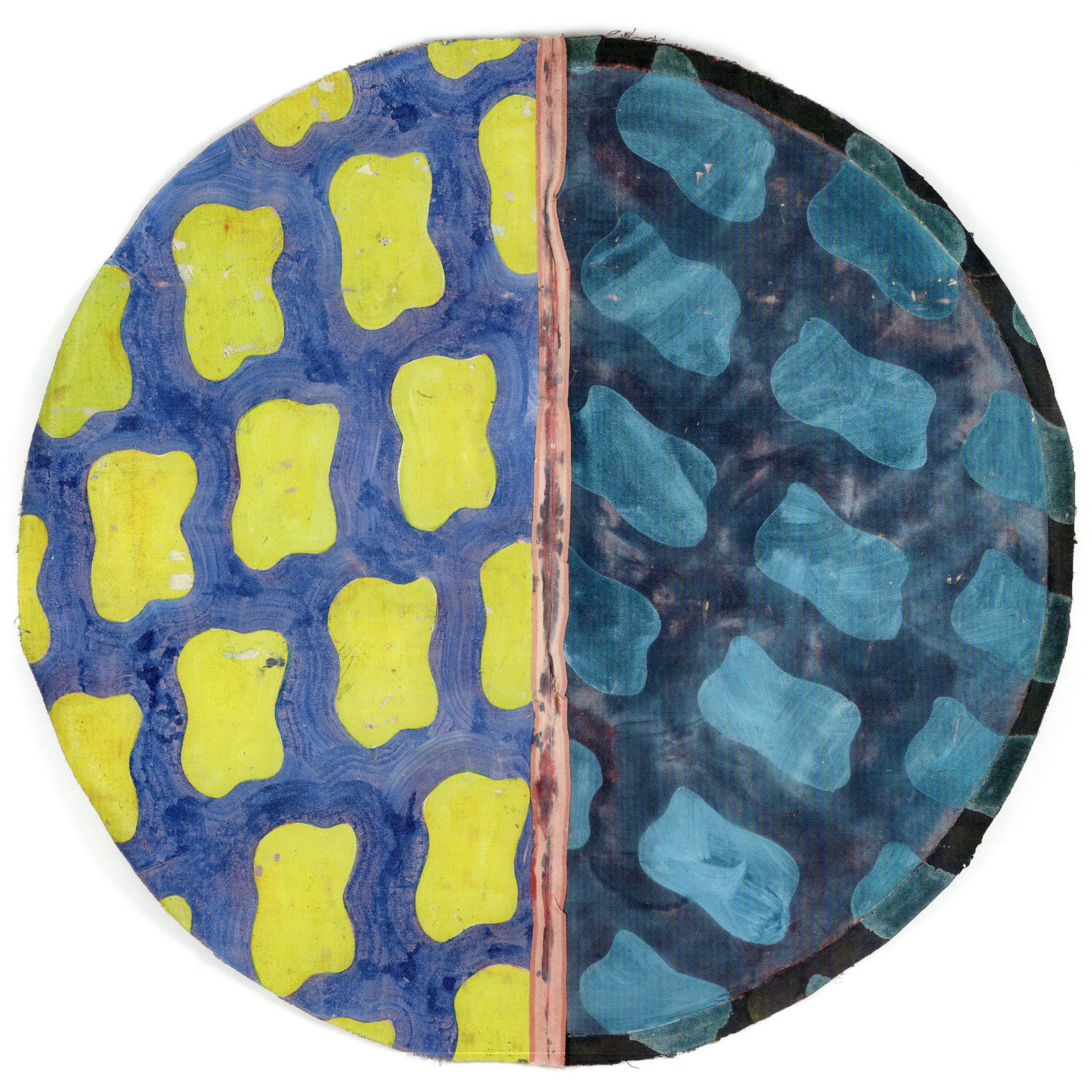

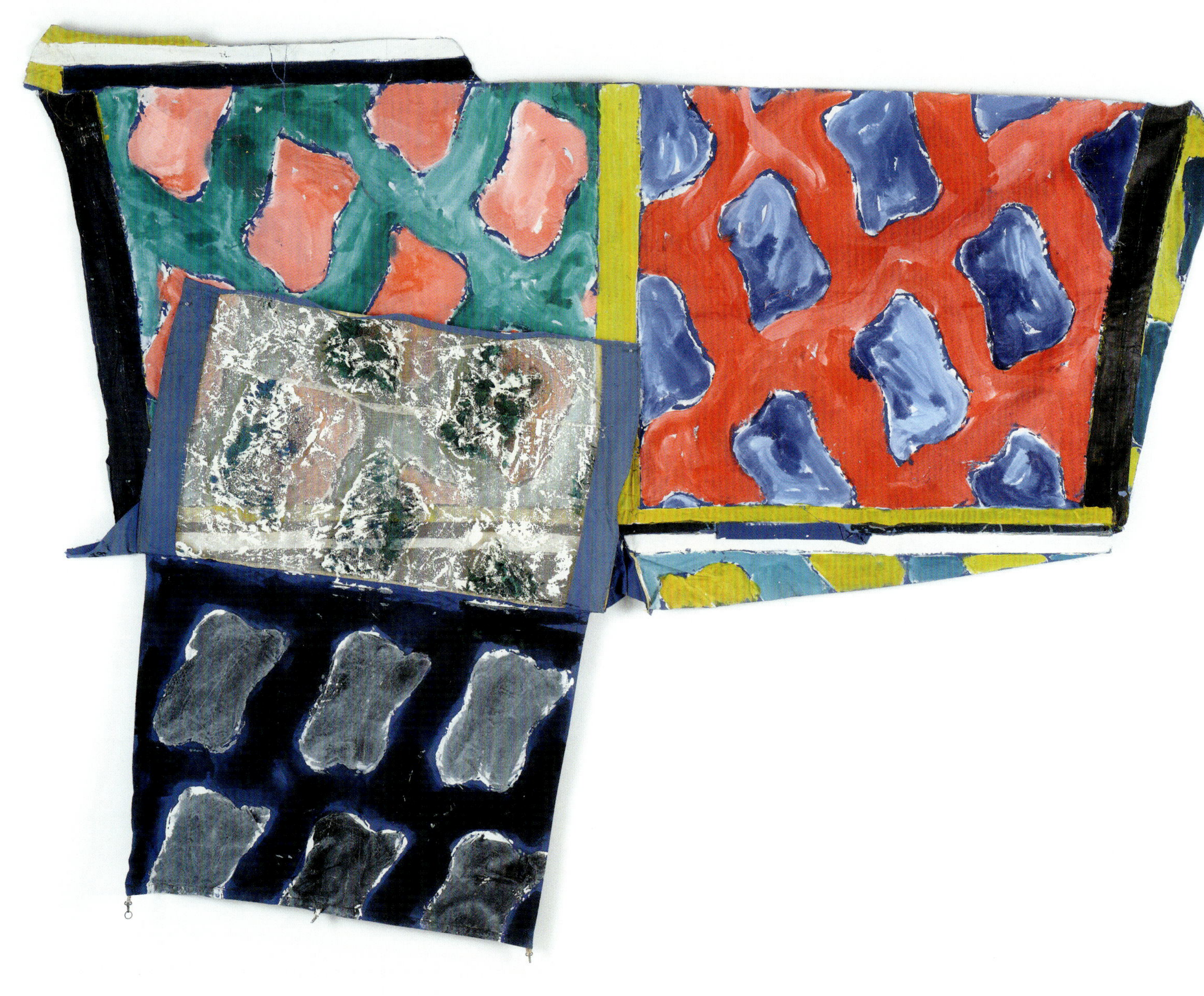

Claude Viallat

1977/024

1977

acrylic on fragment of tent with window made of insect mesh
106 5⁄16 × 83 7⁄8" | 270 × 213 cm

Claude Viallat

1973/026

1973
mordant dye on fabric
99 ⅝ × 78 ¾" | 253 × 200 cm

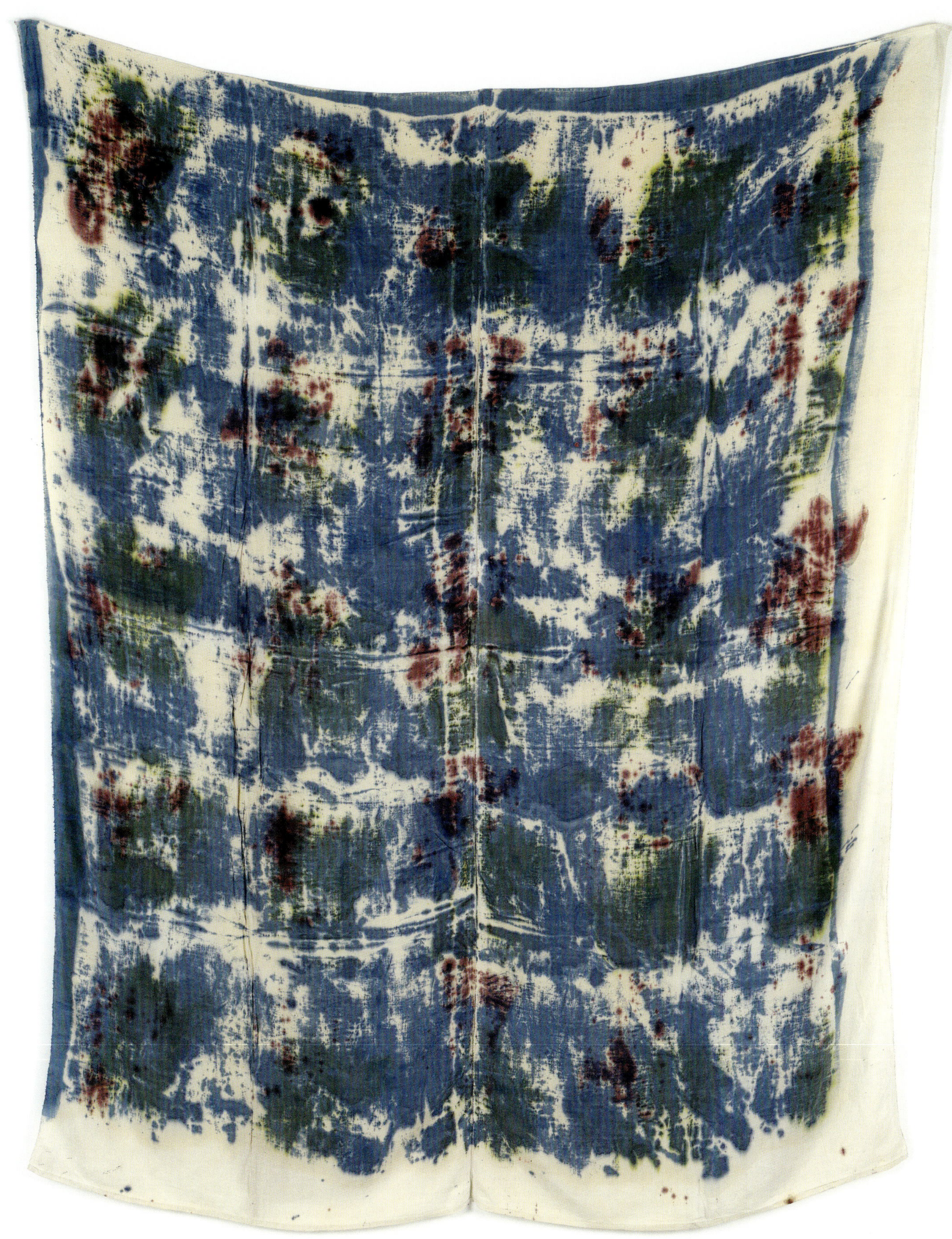

Claude Viallat

1987/OB005

1987

rope and driftwood assemblage

70 ⅞ × 11 ¹³⁄₁₆ × 19 ¹¹⁄₁₆" | 180 × 30 × 50 cm

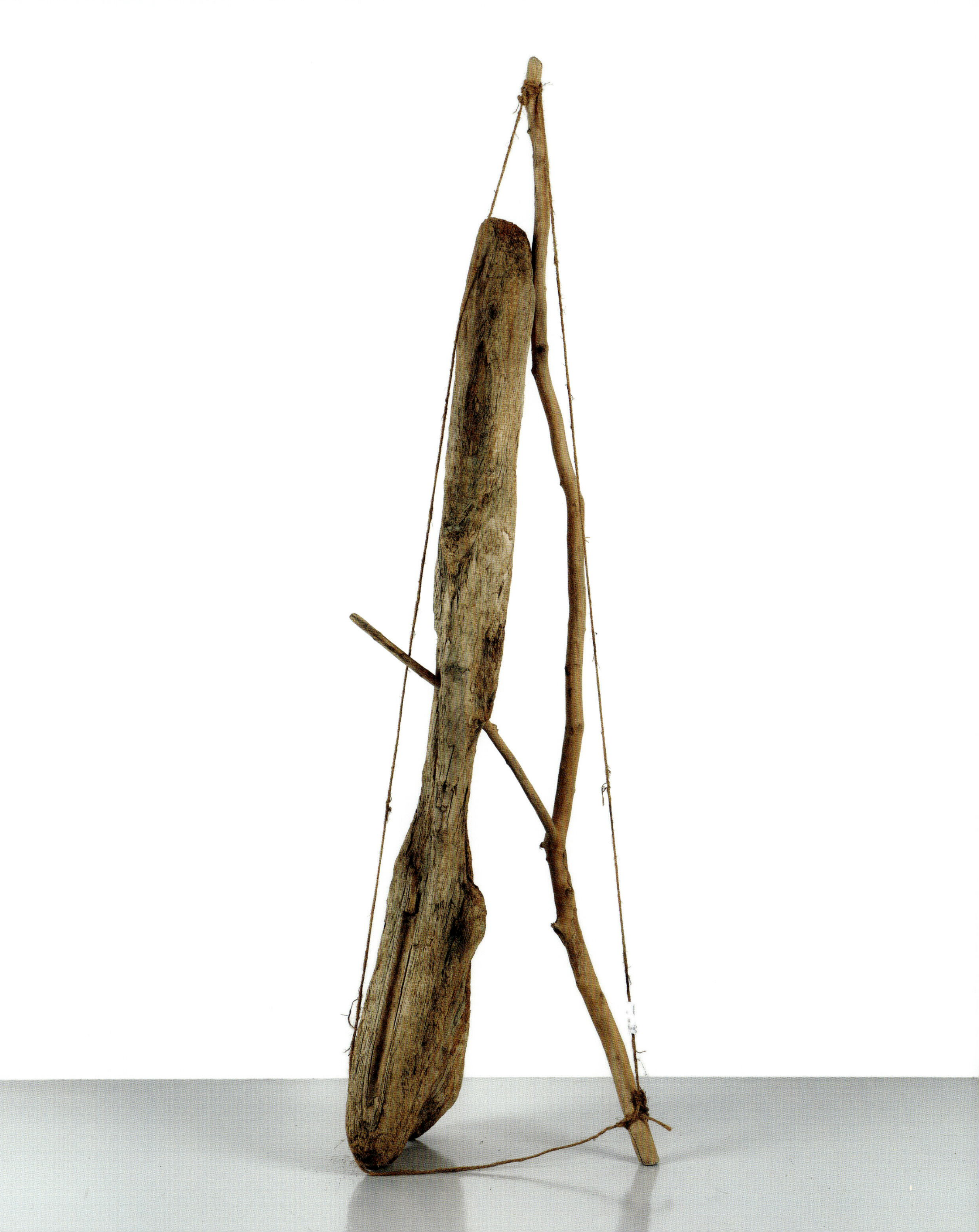

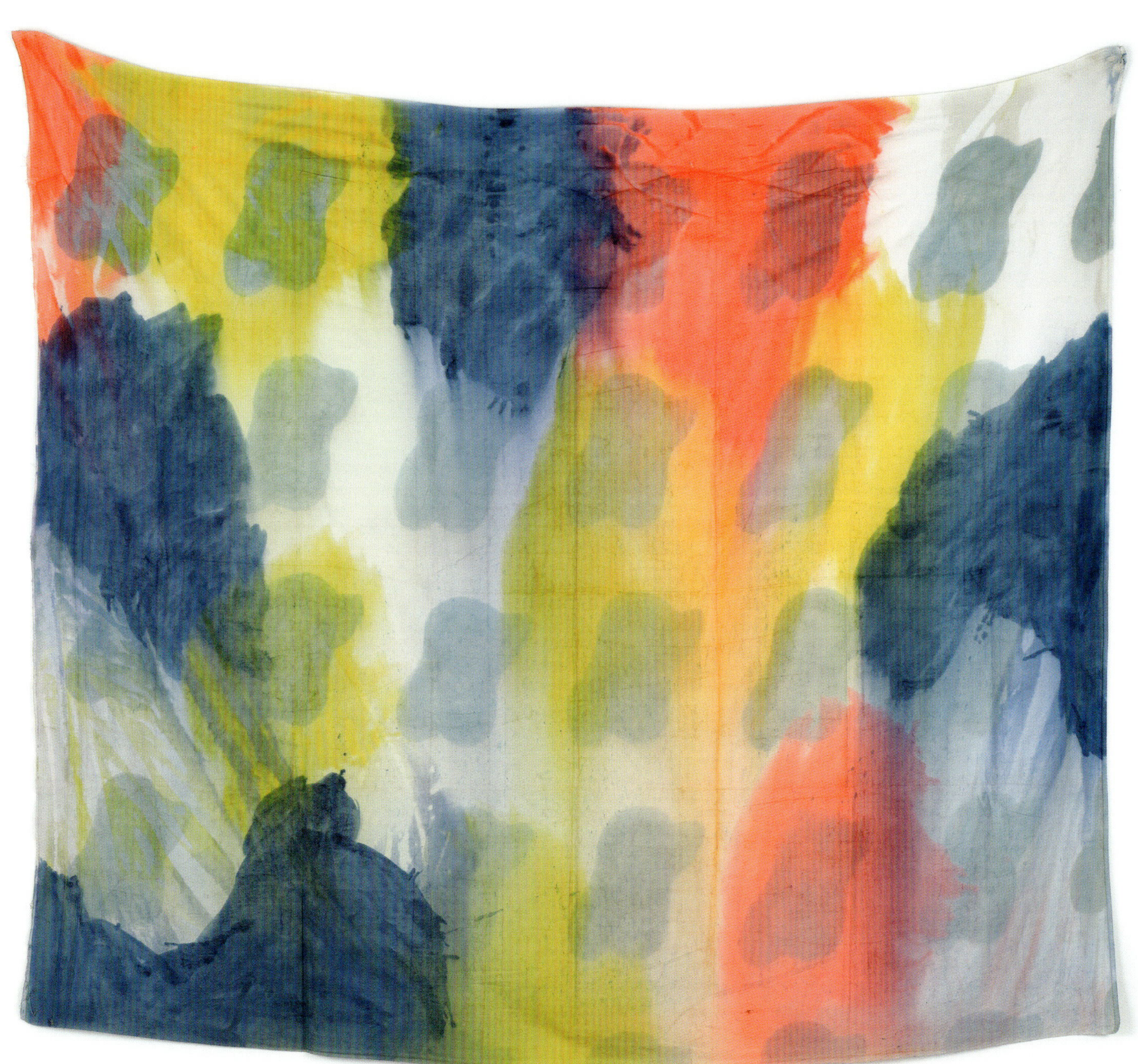

Claude Viallat

1975/023

1975

acrylic on fabric exposed to rain

90 $\frac{9}{16}$ × 82 $\frac{11}{16}$" | 230 × 210 cm

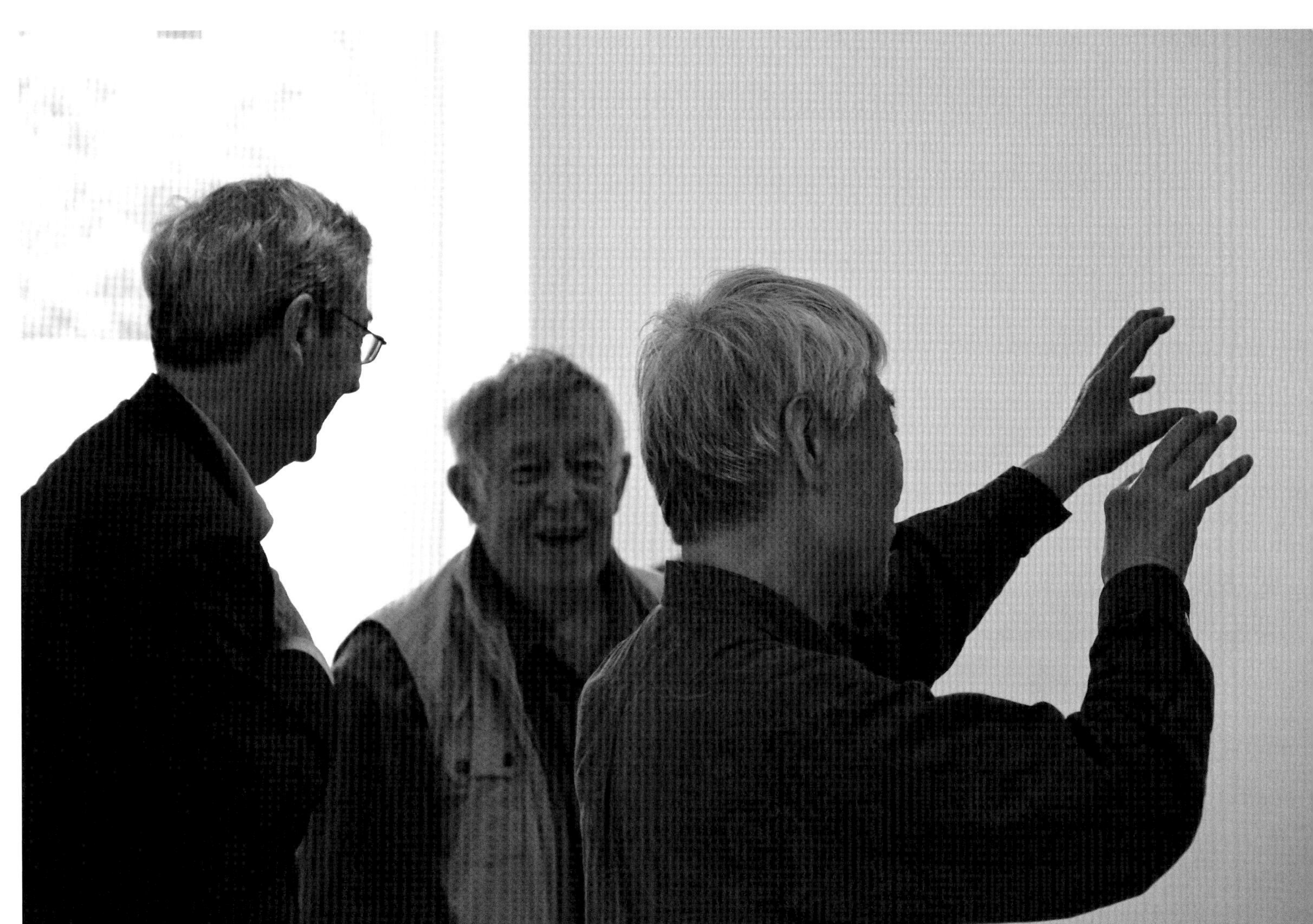

A lecture on the end of easel painting delivered at the École des Beaux-Arts in Montpellier by Lucien Lautrec, a painter who participated in the 1941 Paris exhibition *Vingt jeunes peintres de tradition française (Twenty Young Painters in the French Tradition)* with Jean René Bazaine and Alfred Manessier, was very important to me. Then I came to the awareness of the "outsized" American paintings and working with a canvas on the ground and the use of Jackson Pollock's "drip painting." Pollock stepped on the canvas, but along the edges. This oversized nature of American painting could be equated to the scale of the American continent. To this discovery was added Lucio Fontana's puncturing and lacerating of the canvas—opening the scene to its back, its beyond—and then Morris Louis's dripping of the paint onto the plane of the canvas. My work, our work, could not help but to be impacted and deviate from the academic conventions and the French artistic scene.

But no one was interested in our work. We had to present it ourselves, and it could only be done by us. Therefore, we could present it anywhere. Nothing prevented us from presenting it in space. Nothing prevented us from placing it on the ground. We were free to discard representation, perspective, the horizon line, etc.

The materiality of the canvas became an asset. Folding and crumpling did not take anything away from it, but became technical options for development . . .

And any presentation contributed to modifying and opening up the work. Systematic creation was linked to presentation, and they were analyzed together. The resulting image had no other importance than to be read in words and actions.

The initial definition of the support, its use, could be taken into account or not. All the components of the work will act and must be accepted, regulated, and obviously mobilized or emphasized.

I remember certain Mono-ha pieces at the Musée d'Art Moderne de Paris during the 1969 Biennale de Paris: a canvas repeating the same artistic gesture six or seven times, a rectangular mesh placed on the ground with its links extended.

We exhibited works—Daniel Dezeuze, Patrick Saytour, and myself—at the entrance to the Palais Galliera. Daniel showed a frame, a 100 F format, with a walnut stain; Patrick showed a white canvas with marked folds creating a grid; and I showed a sheet stamped with blue shapes and a net with blue knots that was about 2 by 2 meters.

On the ground to the side, Ben Vautier had placed a string of packages, making a grid, more or less, a small stretcher, and a mirror, all of them from the 1960s.

Seeing Lee Ufan's work at the following Biennial in 1971—the glass plate shattered by a stone—was a revelation to me, a simple act modifying a material with such efficiency and proposing, at the same time as the reading following the act, a fixed scattering; it was truly a suspended moment.

From there, how could we open the reading of things to modify them and arrive at an act of pure simplicity to create such an obvious result?

Of course the result is definitive and enduring. How can we read and link simple things that can be easily replaced? The extended mesh and repetition of alike objects was easier for me, especially since I had addressed parallel situations.

But the glass broken by the stone?

I think I had wrestled with the problem for a long time, and I encountered it several times afterwards, getting close to it but not solving it. Today there is still an ongoing transgression to be challenged and, in the wanderings of my work beyond painting, a de facto line that is always in the distance.

Claude V
017d1968,
ink on p
8 ¼ × 6 11⁄16" | 21 ×

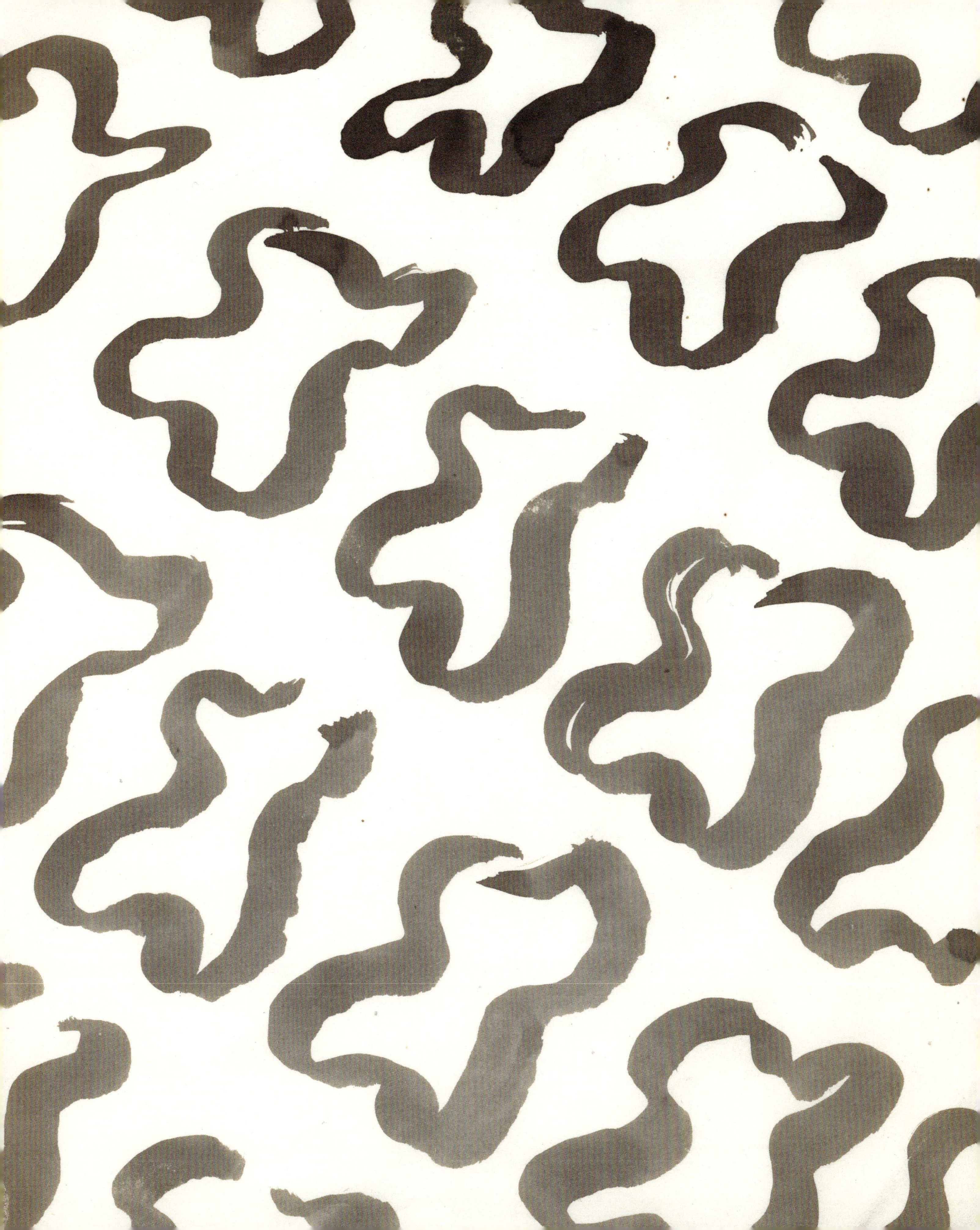

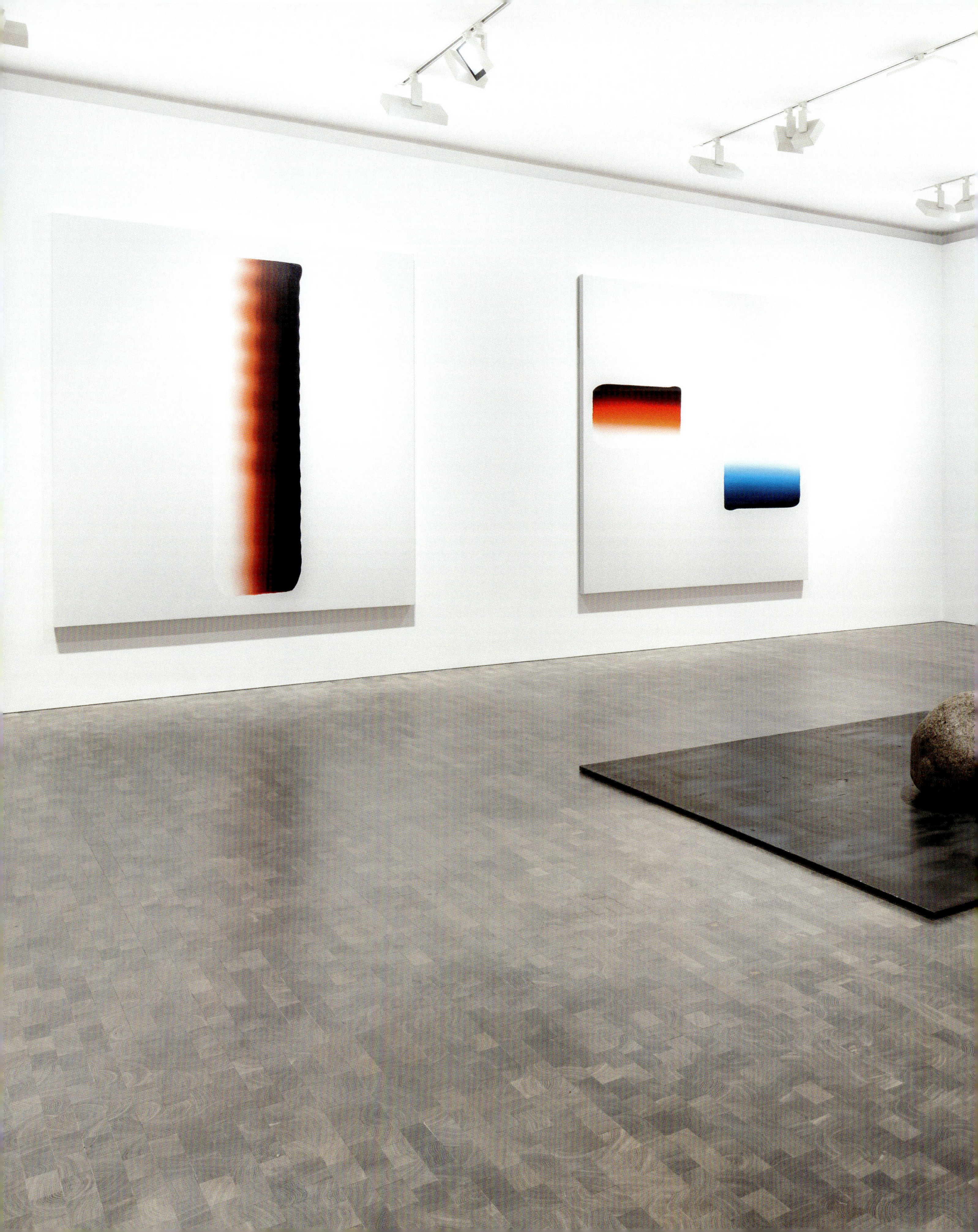

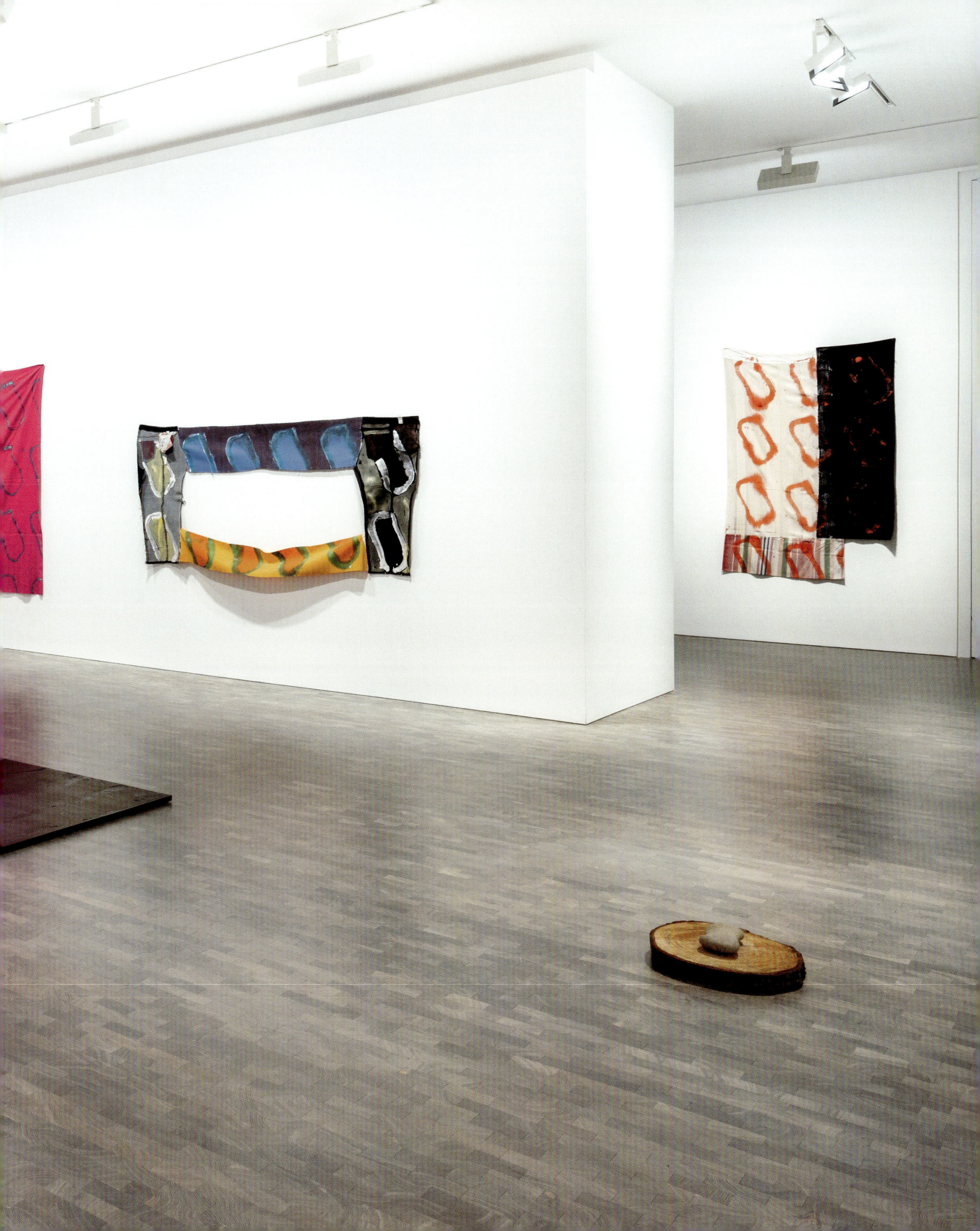

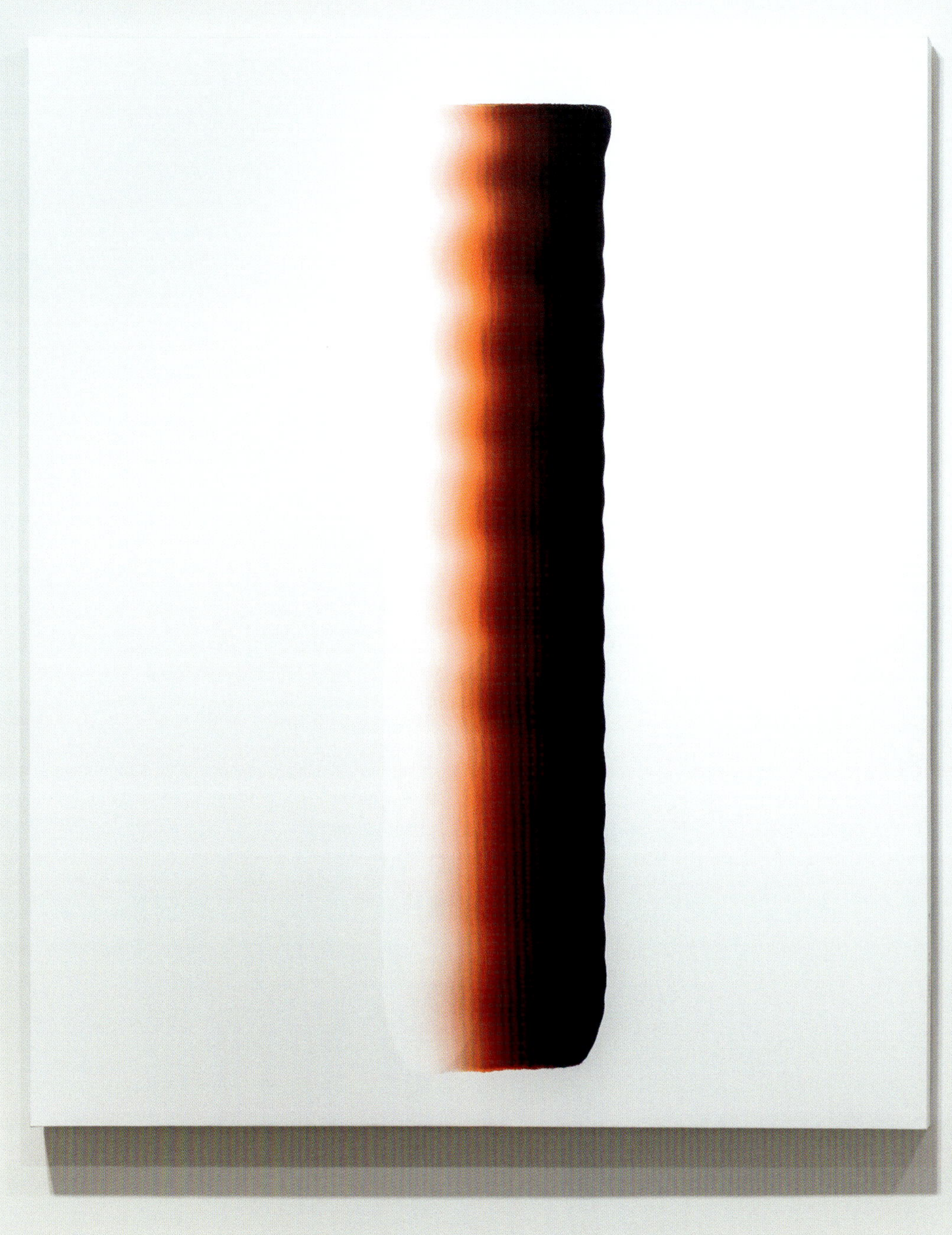

Lee Ufan

RESPONSE

2023
acrylic on canvas
89 ⅜ × 71 ⅝" | 227 × 182 cm

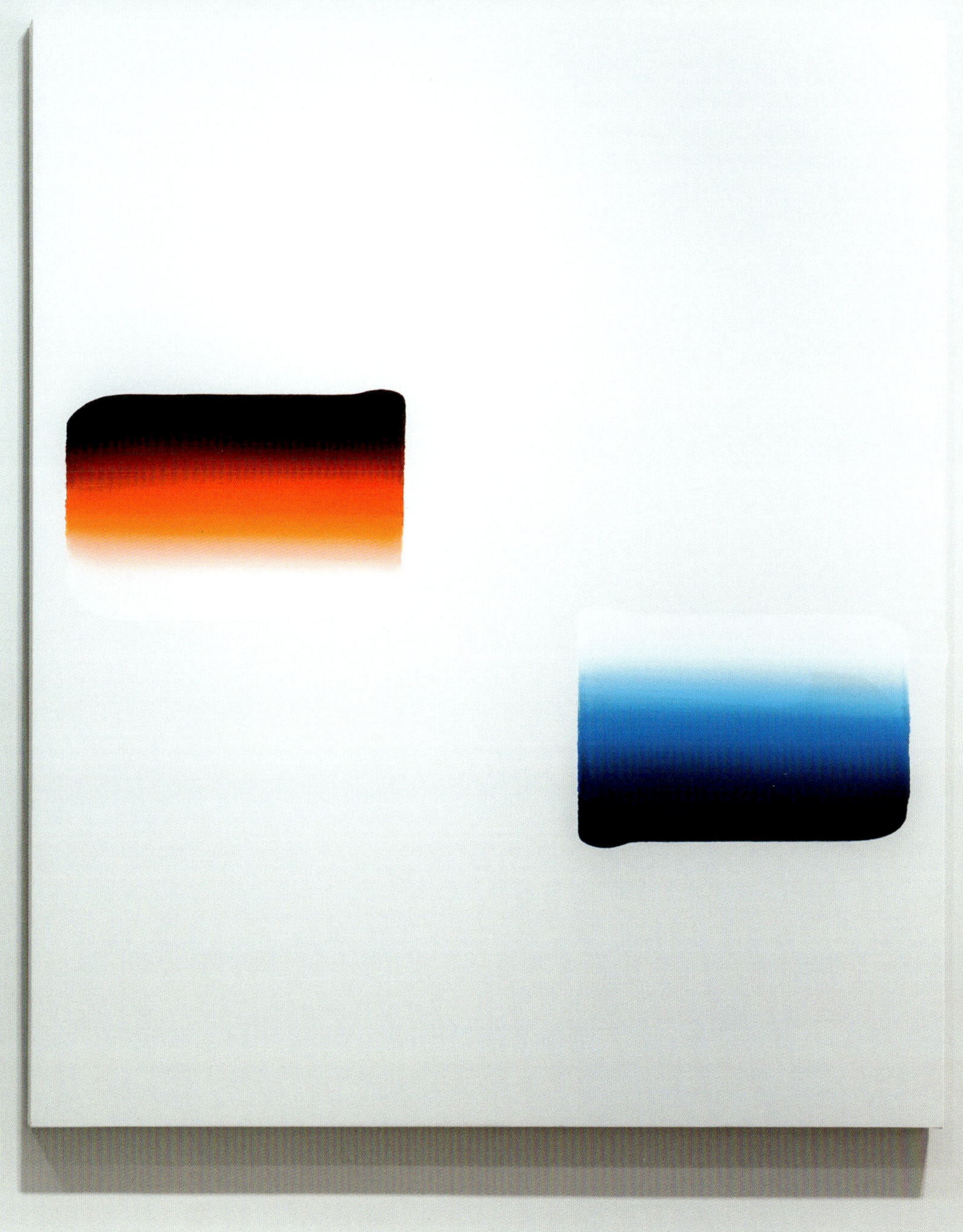

Lee Ufan | **RESPONSE**
2023
acrylic on canvas
89 ⅜ × 71 ⅝" | 227 × 182 cm

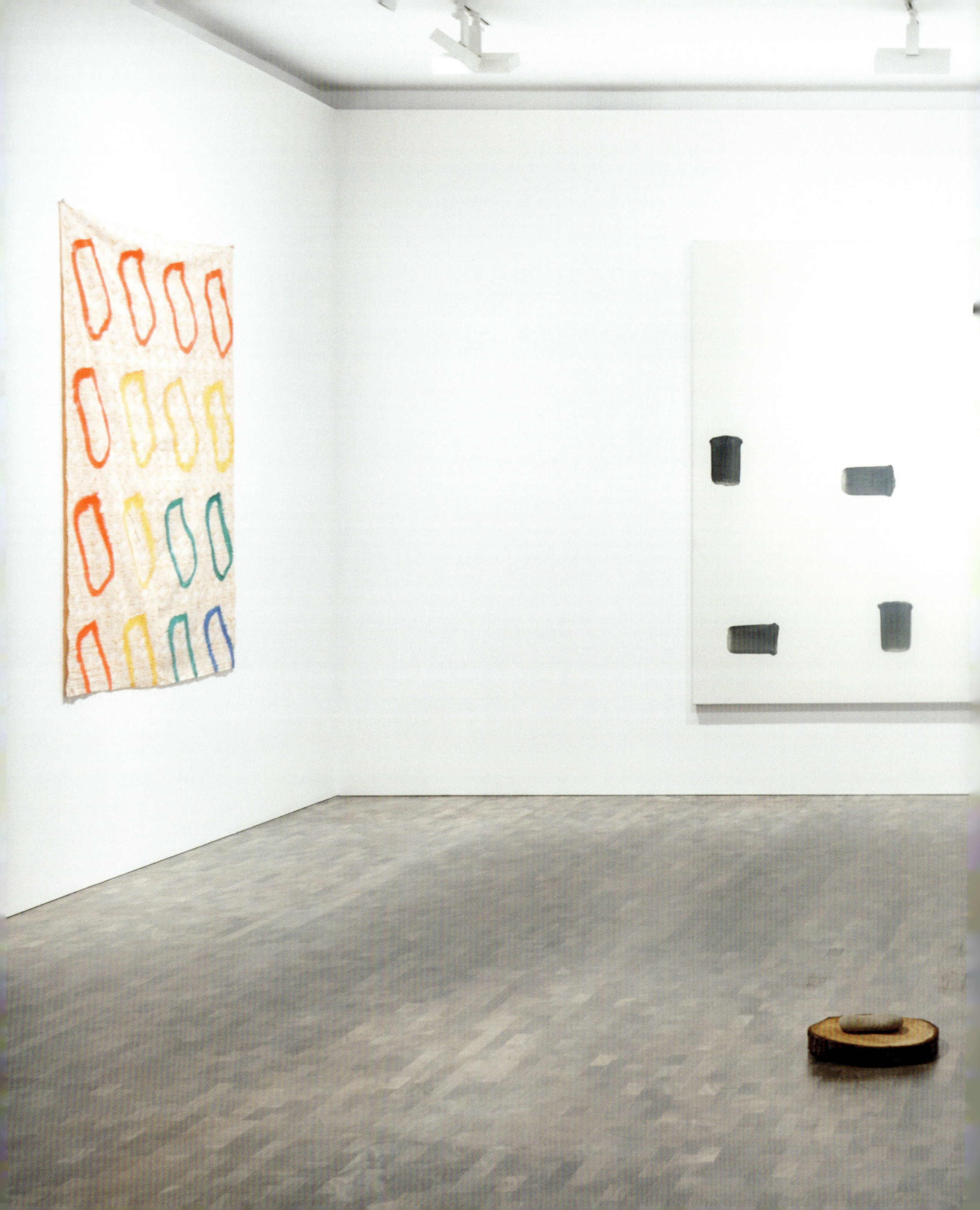

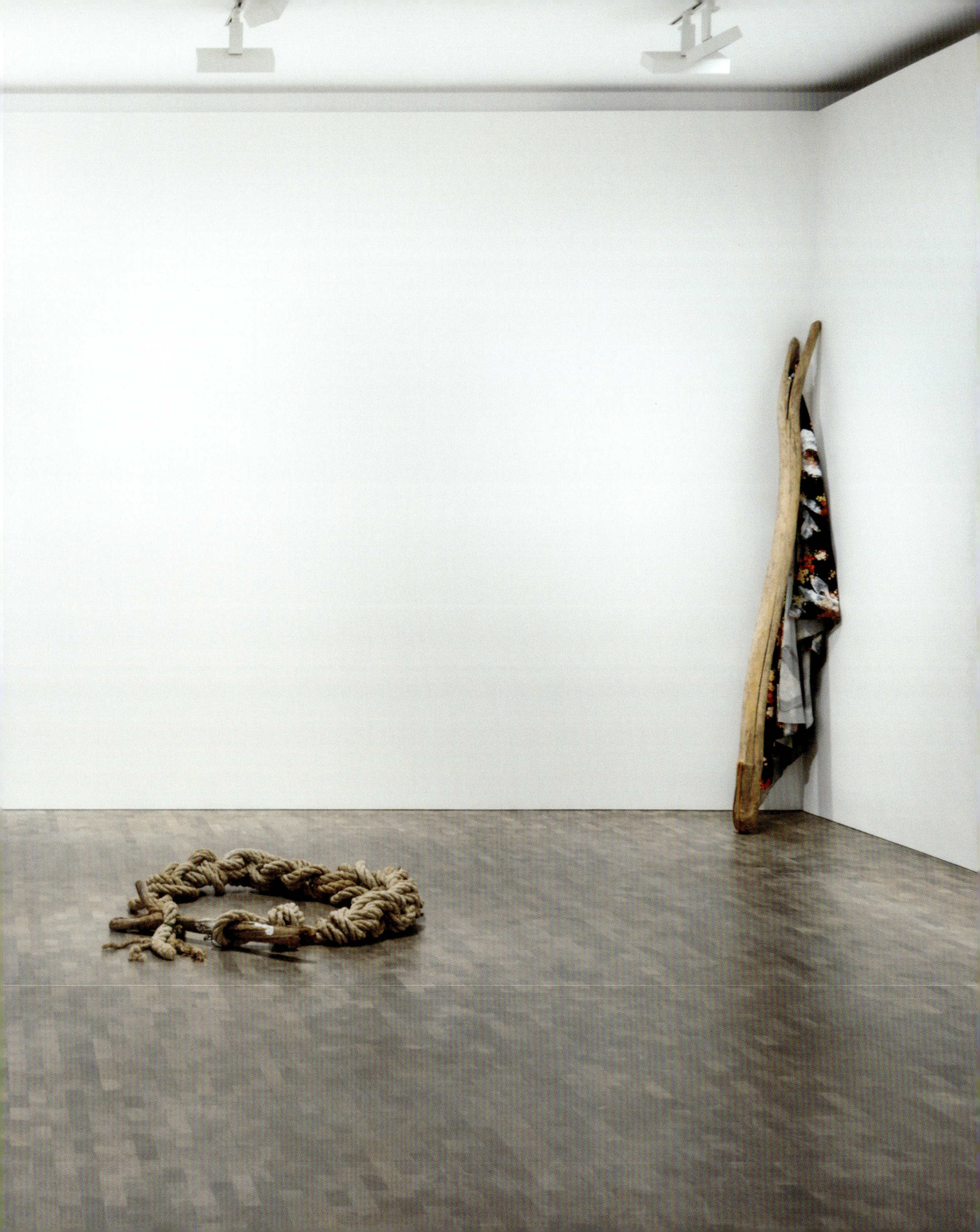

Lee Ufan

CORRESPONDANCE

1992

acrylic on canvas

89 ⅜ × 71 ⅝" | 227 × 181.9 cm

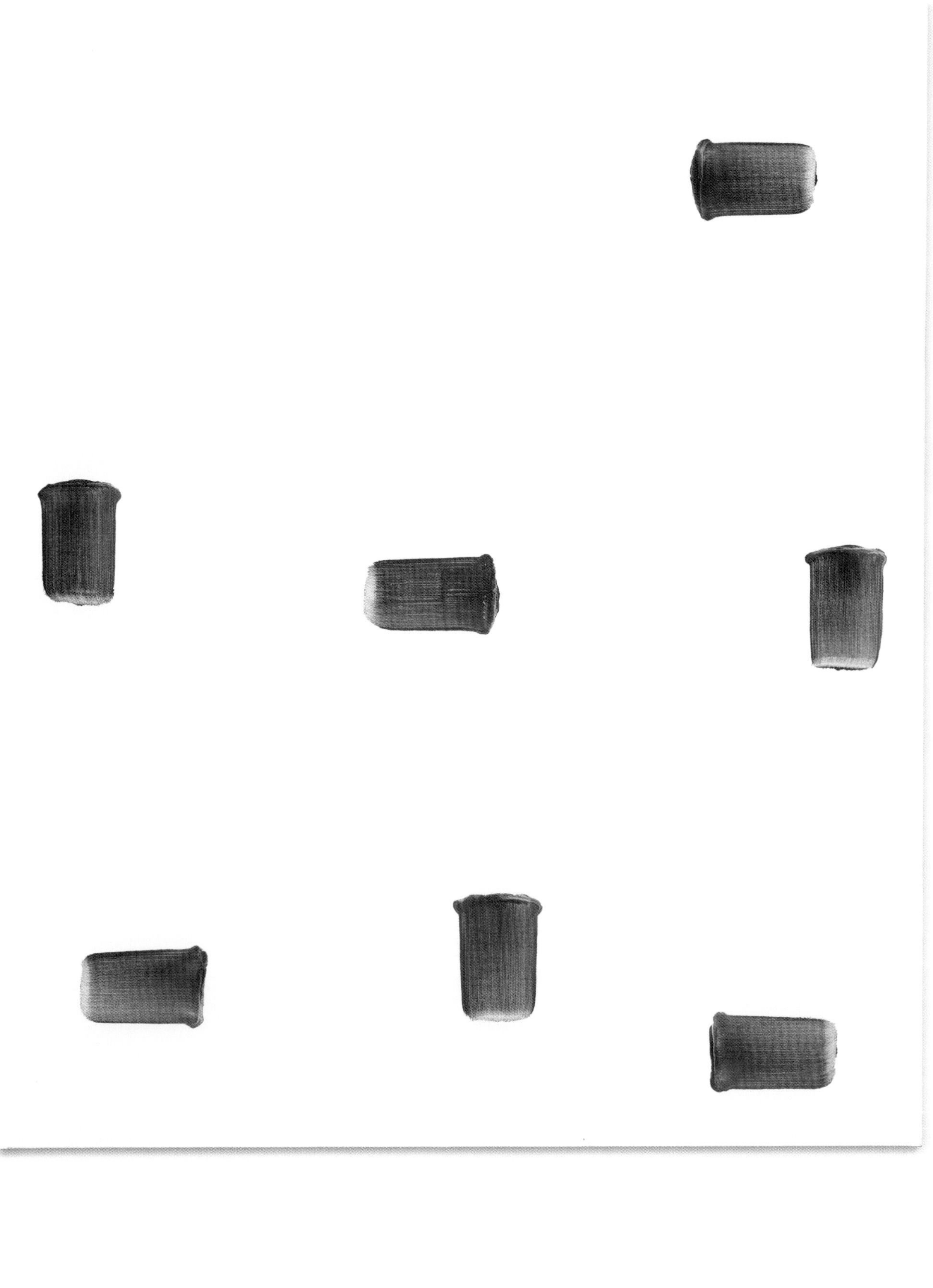

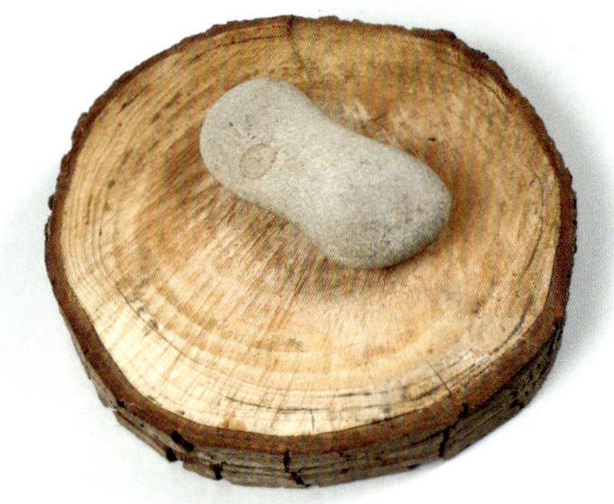

Claude Viallat

2022/OB018 — TRIBUTE TO LEE UFAN

2022
wood and pebble assemblage
diameter 13 ¾" | 34.9 cm

2020/OB026

2020
acrylic on wood and string
39 ⅜ × 31 ½" | 100 × 80 cm

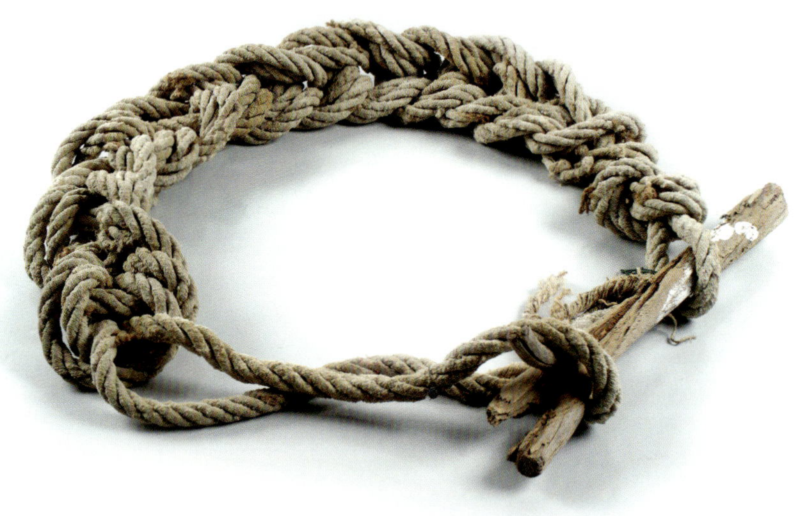

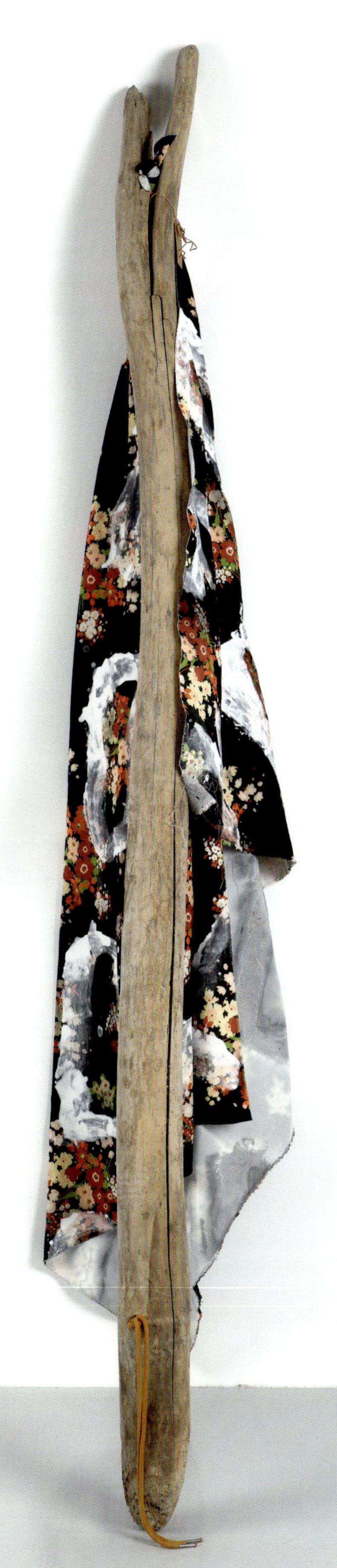

Claude Viallat

2023/OB020

2023
driftwood and acrylic on fabric
96 ⅞ × 5 ⅞" | 246.1 × 14.9 cm

Claude Viallat

2022/124

2022

acrylic on butted fabrics

66 ⅛ × 77 3/16" | 168 × 196.1 cm

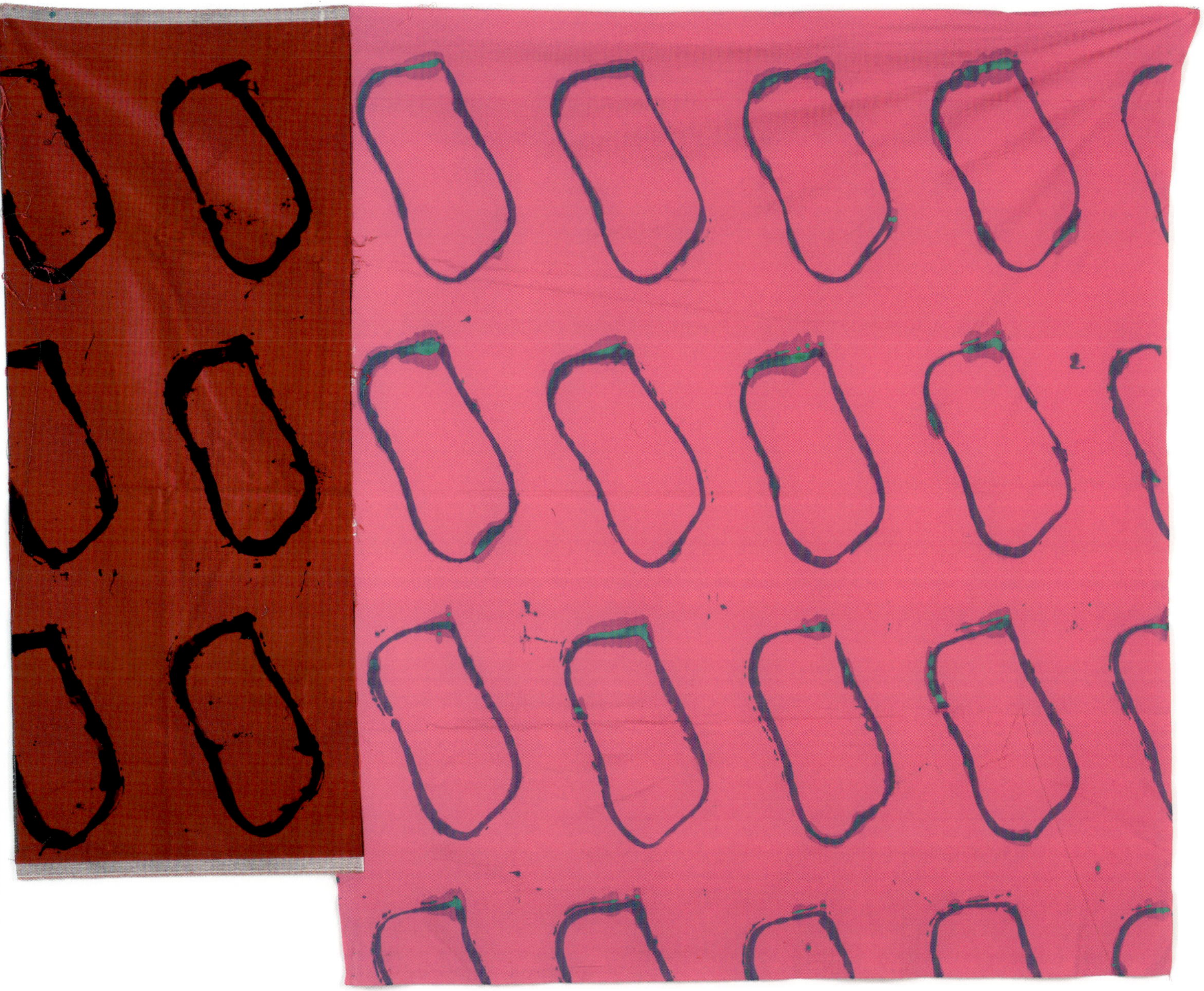

Claude Viallat

2022/119

2022

acrylic on butted fabrics

35 13⁄16 × 76" | 91 × 193 cm

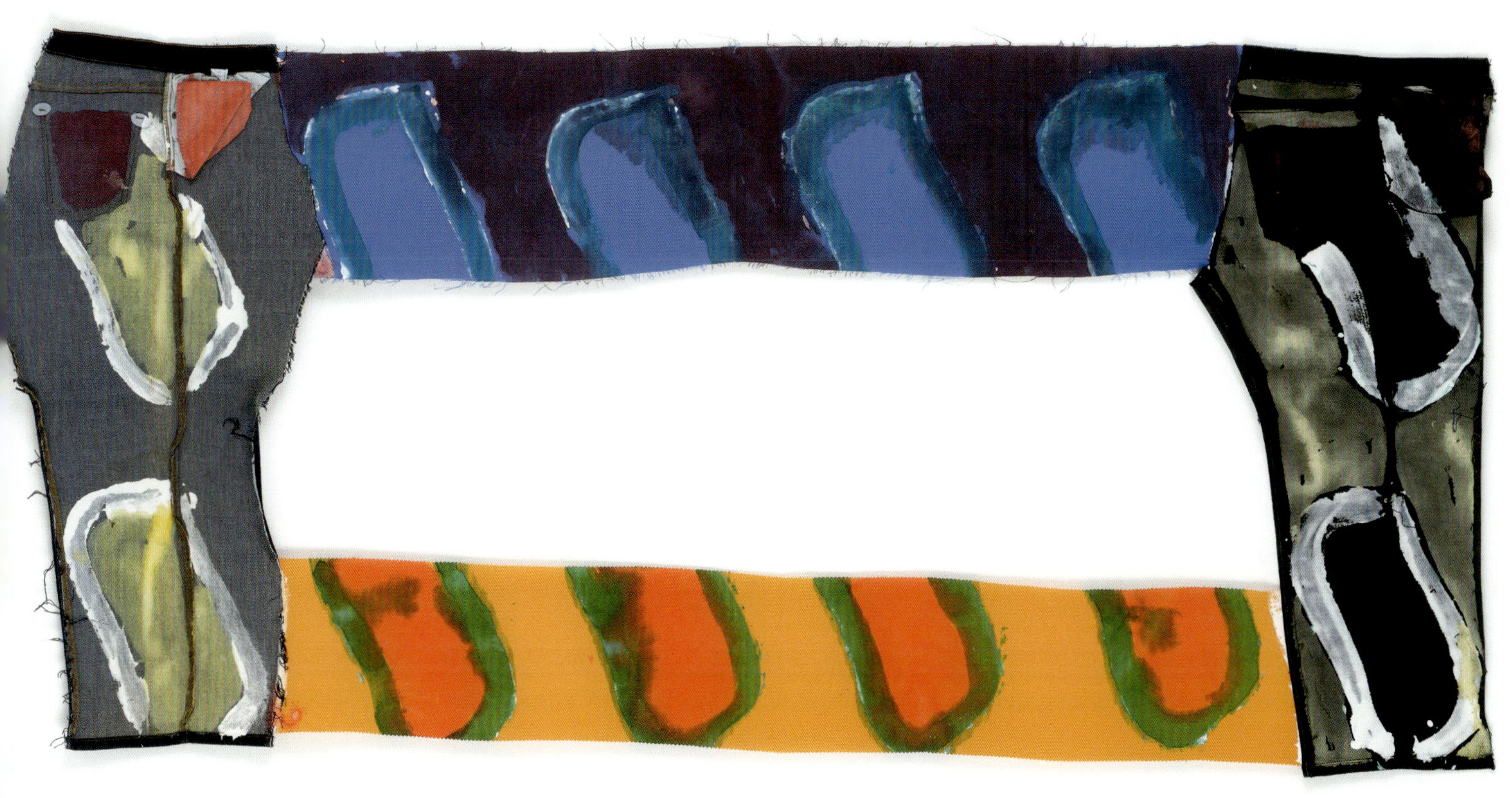

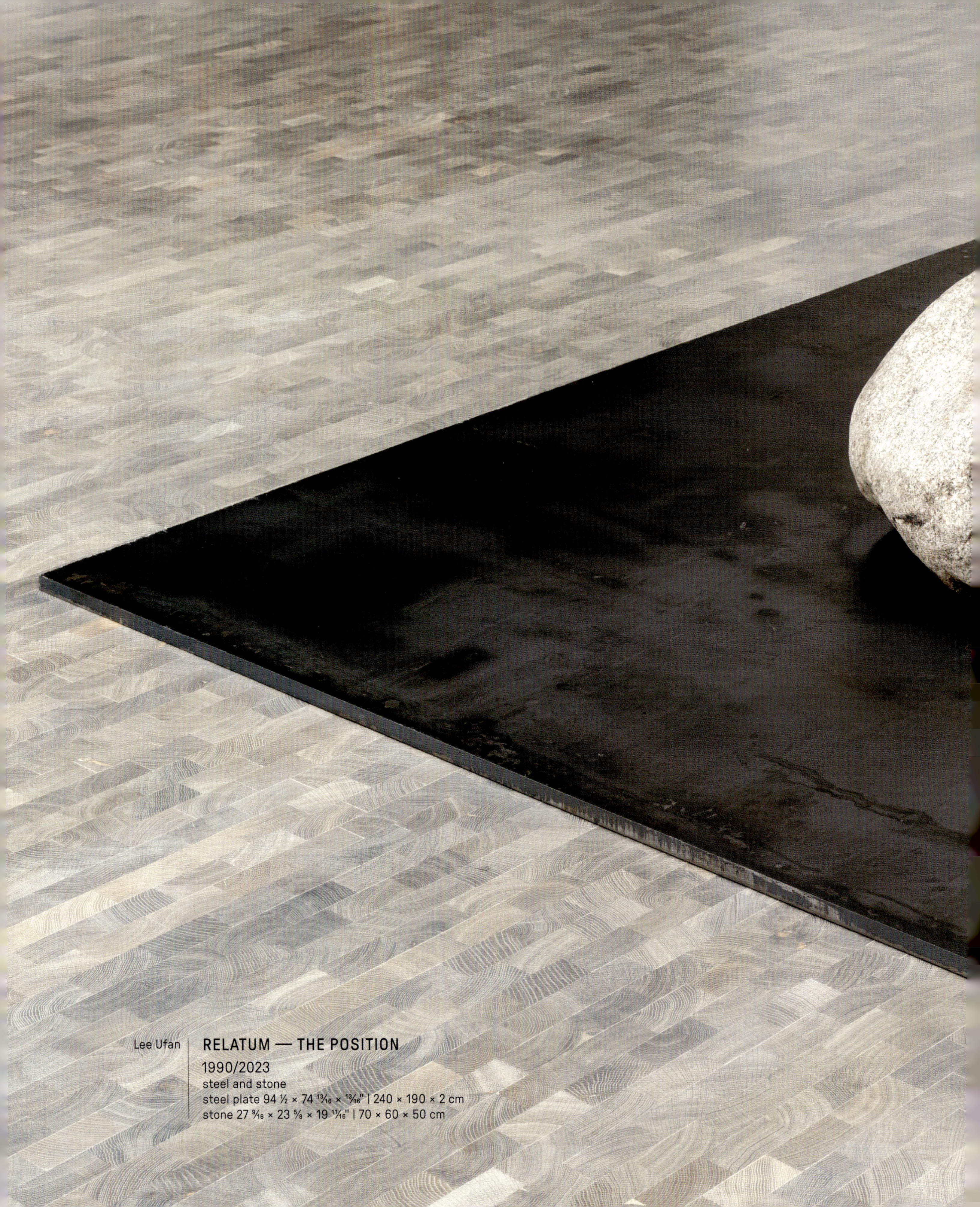

Lee Ufan

RELATUM — THE POSITION

1990/2023
steel and stone
steel plate 94 ½ × 74 13⁄16 × 13⁄16" | 240 × 190 × 2 cm
stone 27 9⁄16 × 23 ⅝ × 19 11⁄16" | 70 × 60 × 50 cm

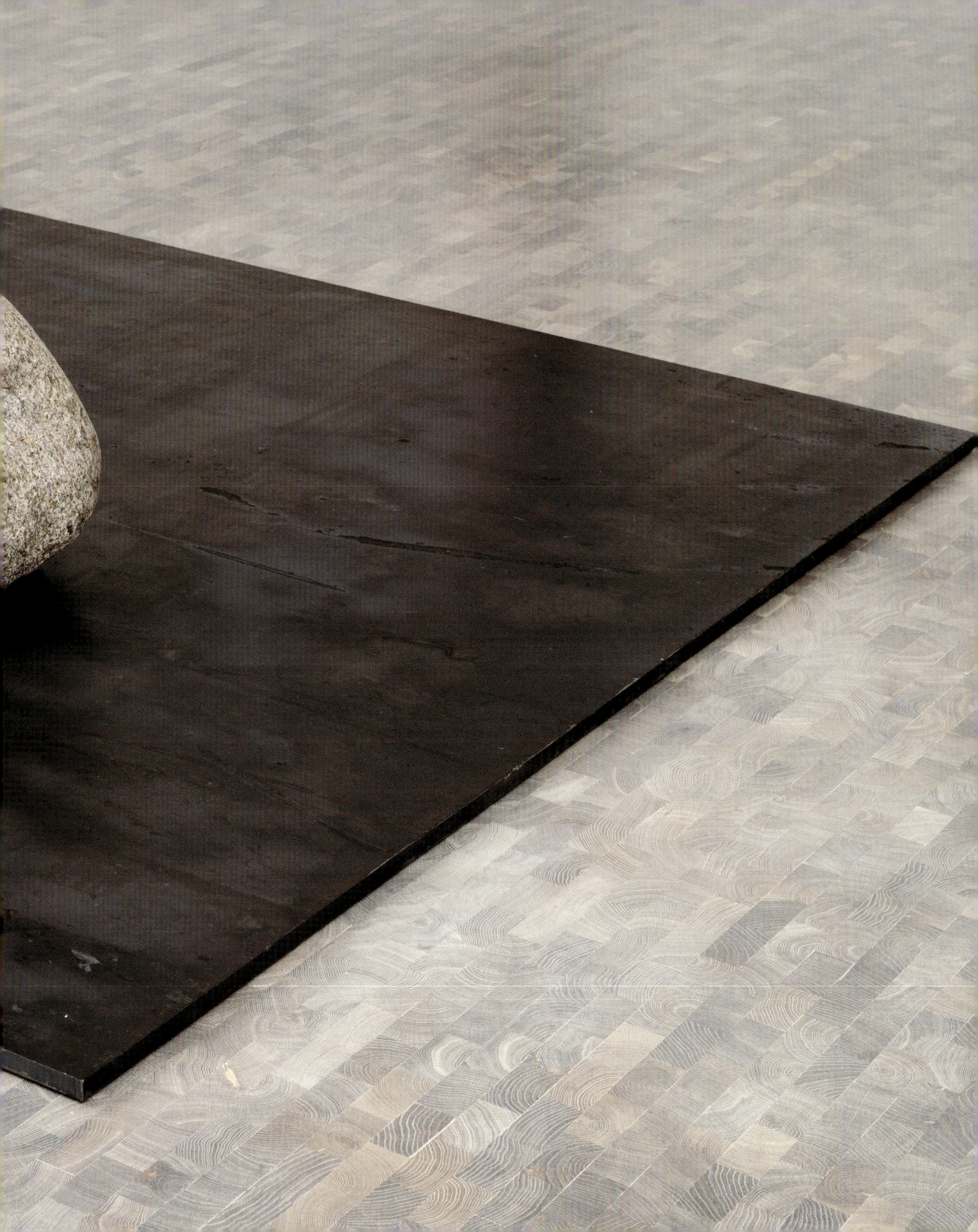

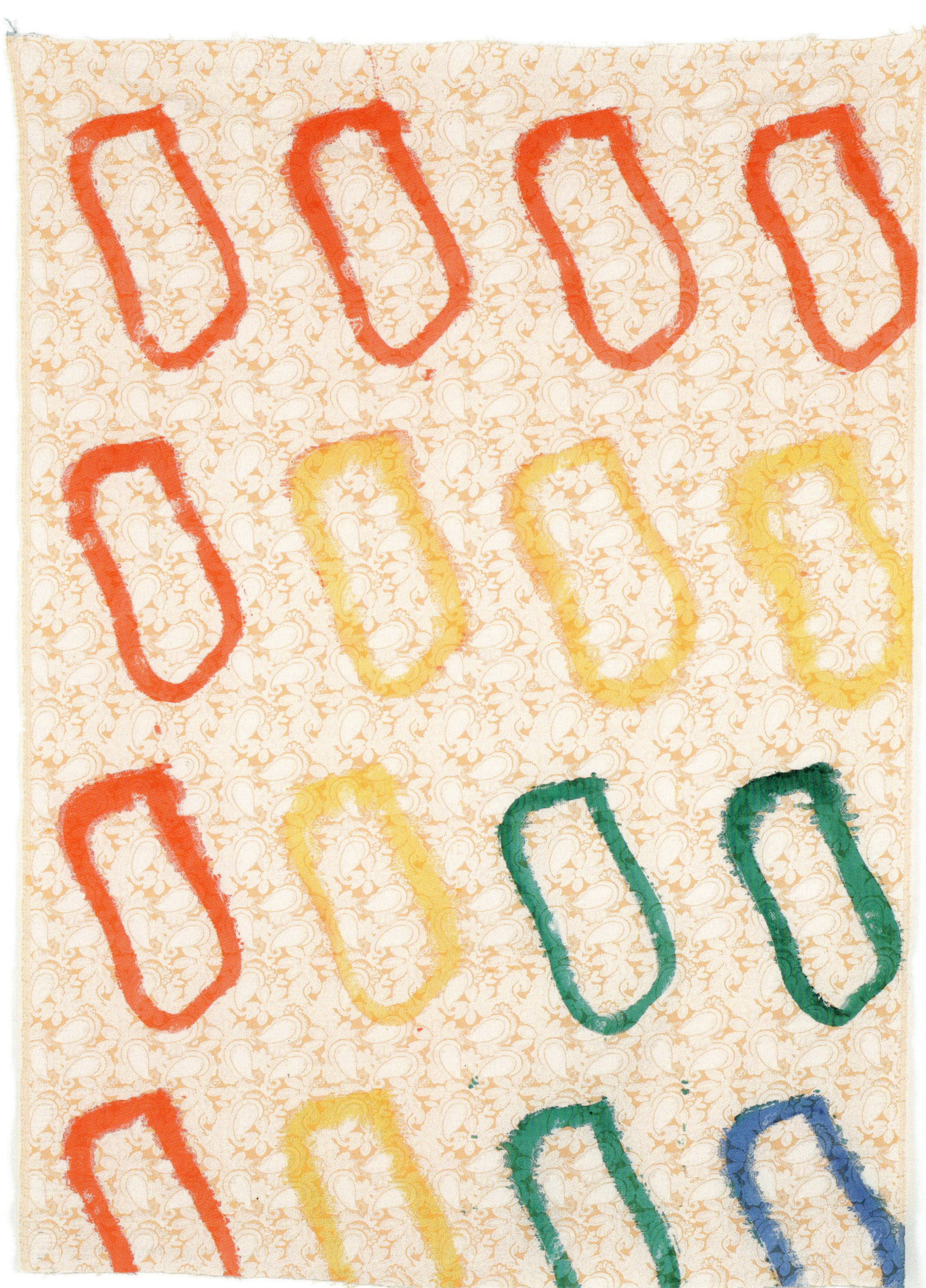

Claude Viallat

2022/115

2022

acrylic on fabric

71 ¼ × 50 ¹³⁄₁₆" | 181 × 129.1 cm

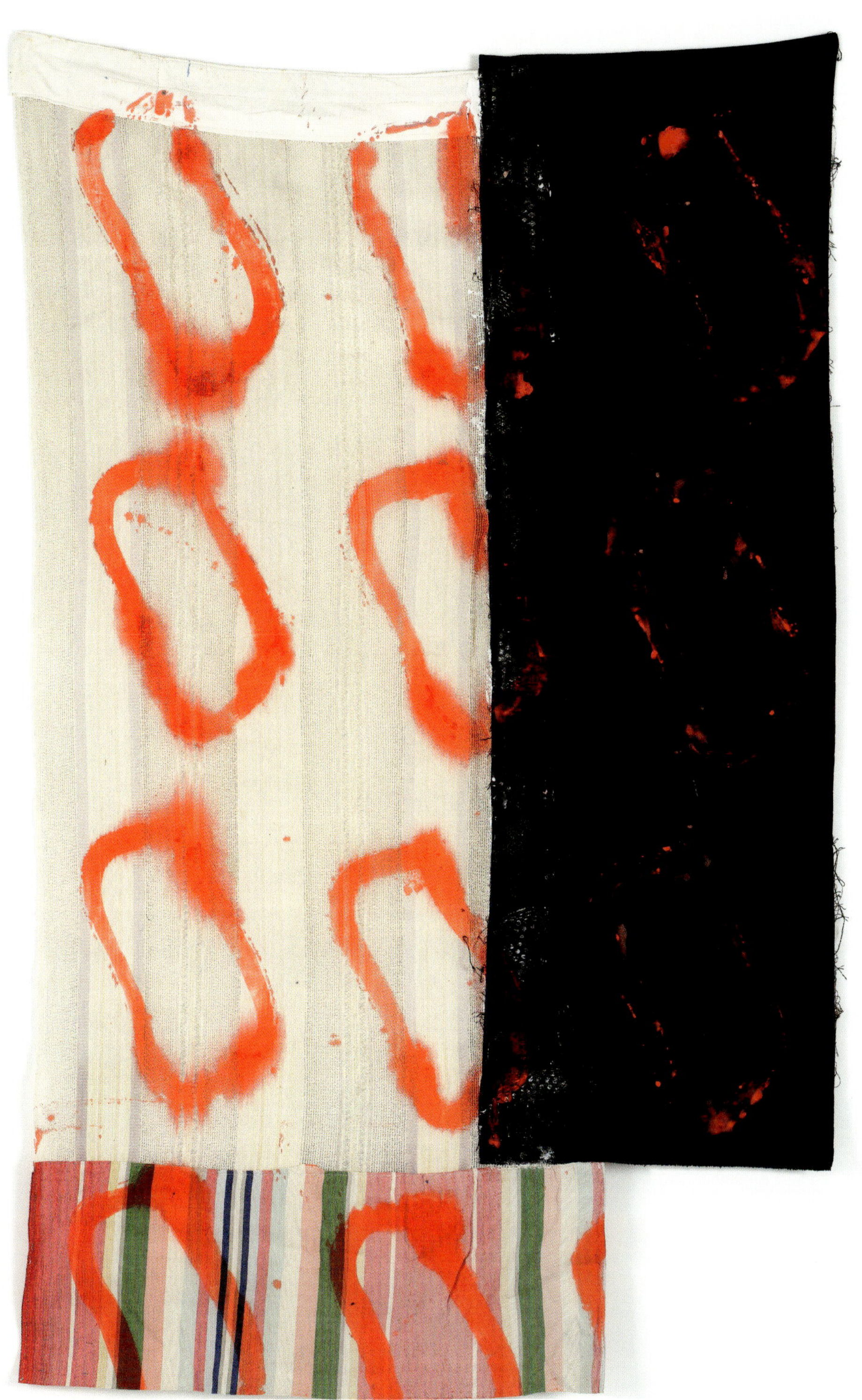

Claude Viallat

2022/138

2022

acrylic on butted fabrics

69 ⁵⁄₁₆ × 40 ⁹⁄₁₆" | 176.1 × 103 cm

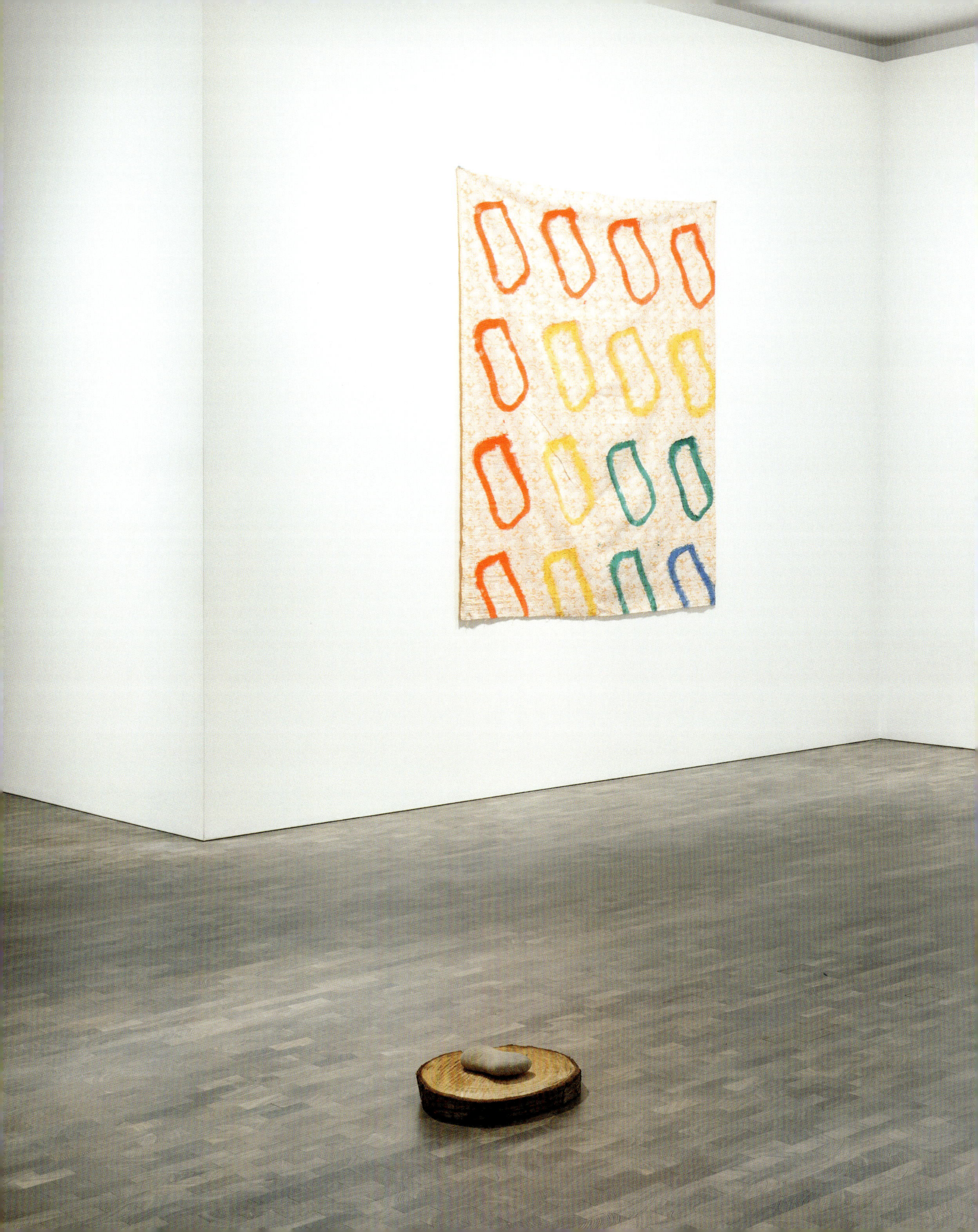

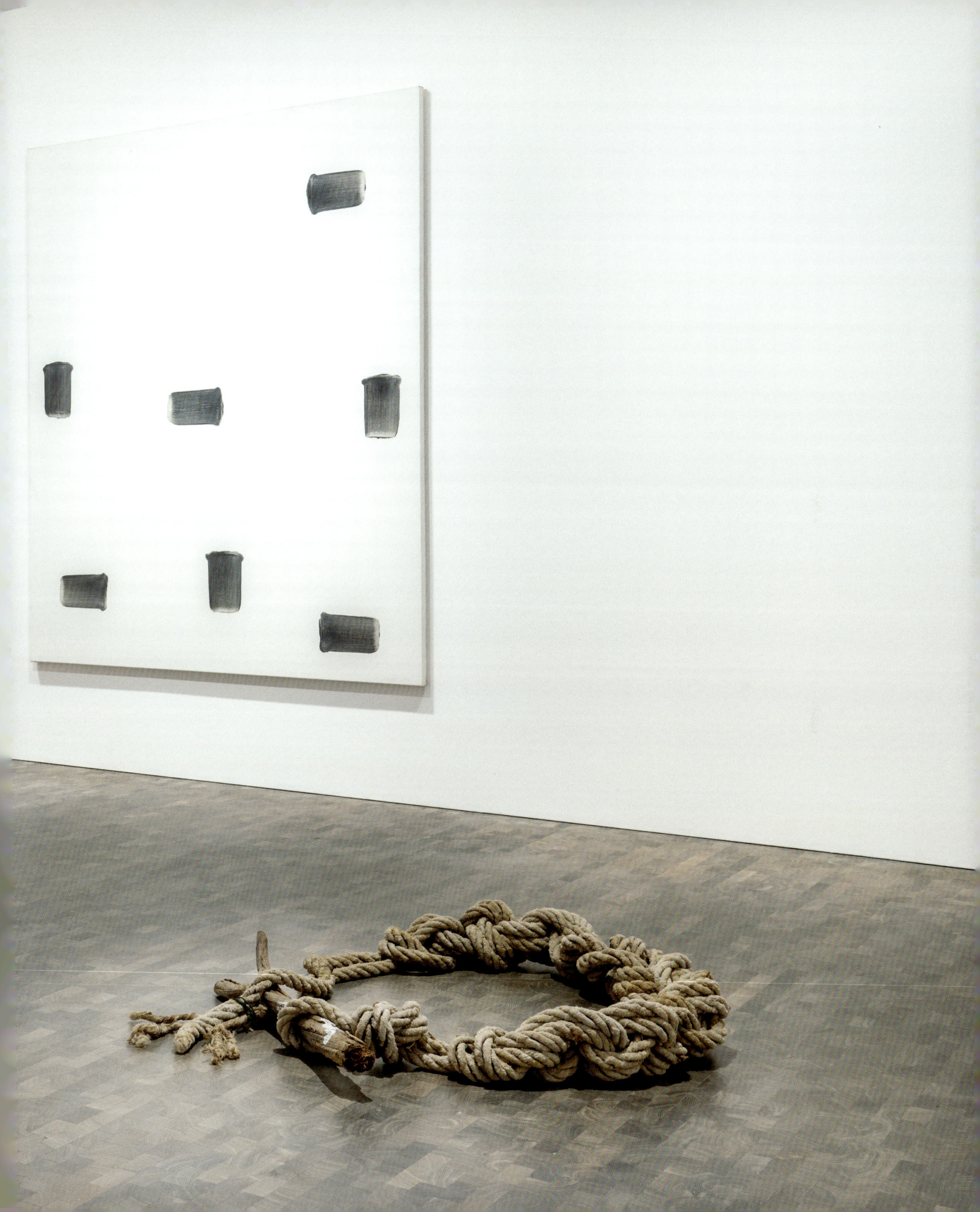

Claude Viallat

2022/184

2022

acrylic on parasol canvas

diameter 68 ⅞" | 174.9 cm

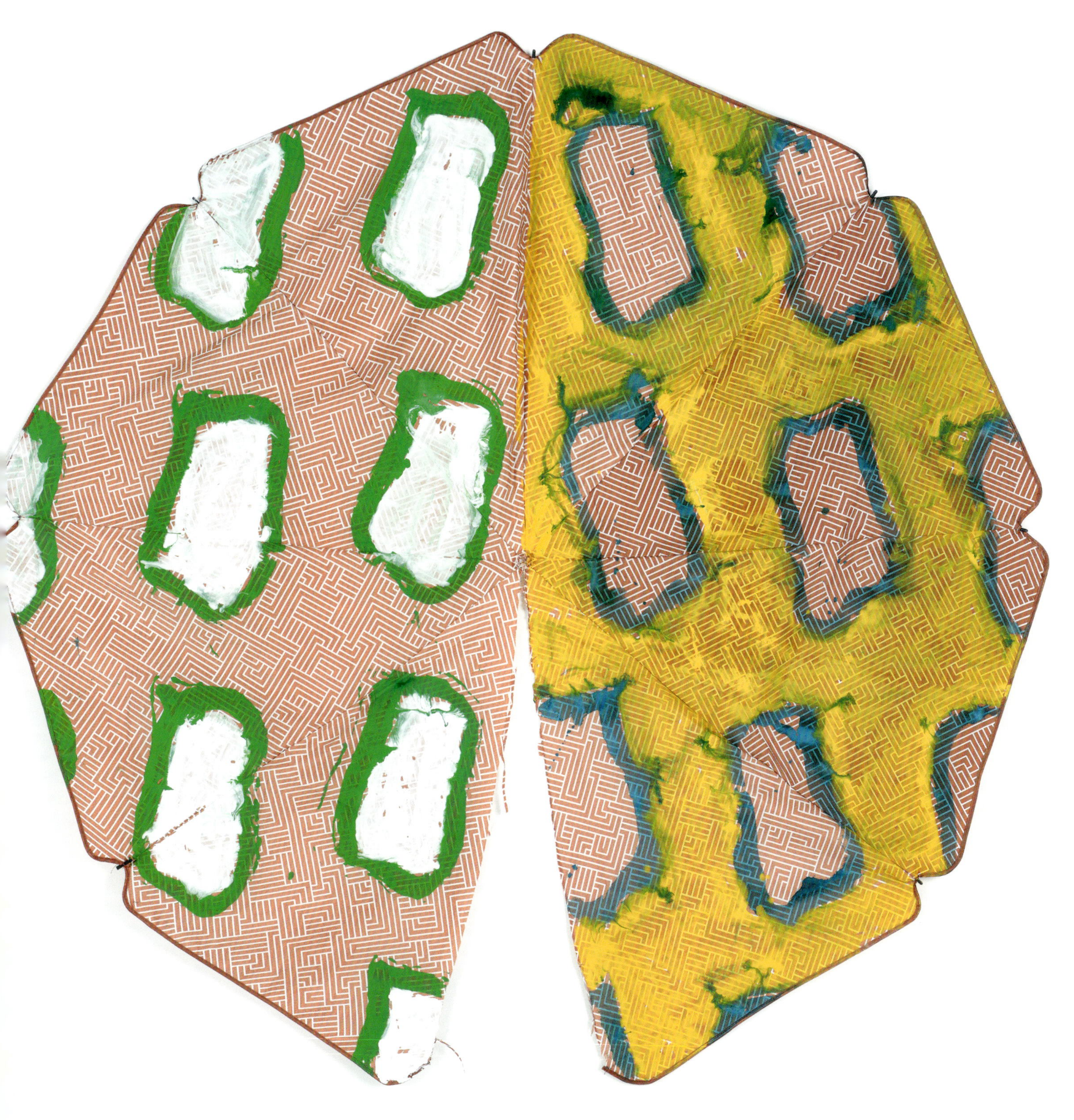

Claude Viallat

1974/027

1974
mordant dye on white sheet
109 7/16 × 81 ½" | 278 × 207 cm

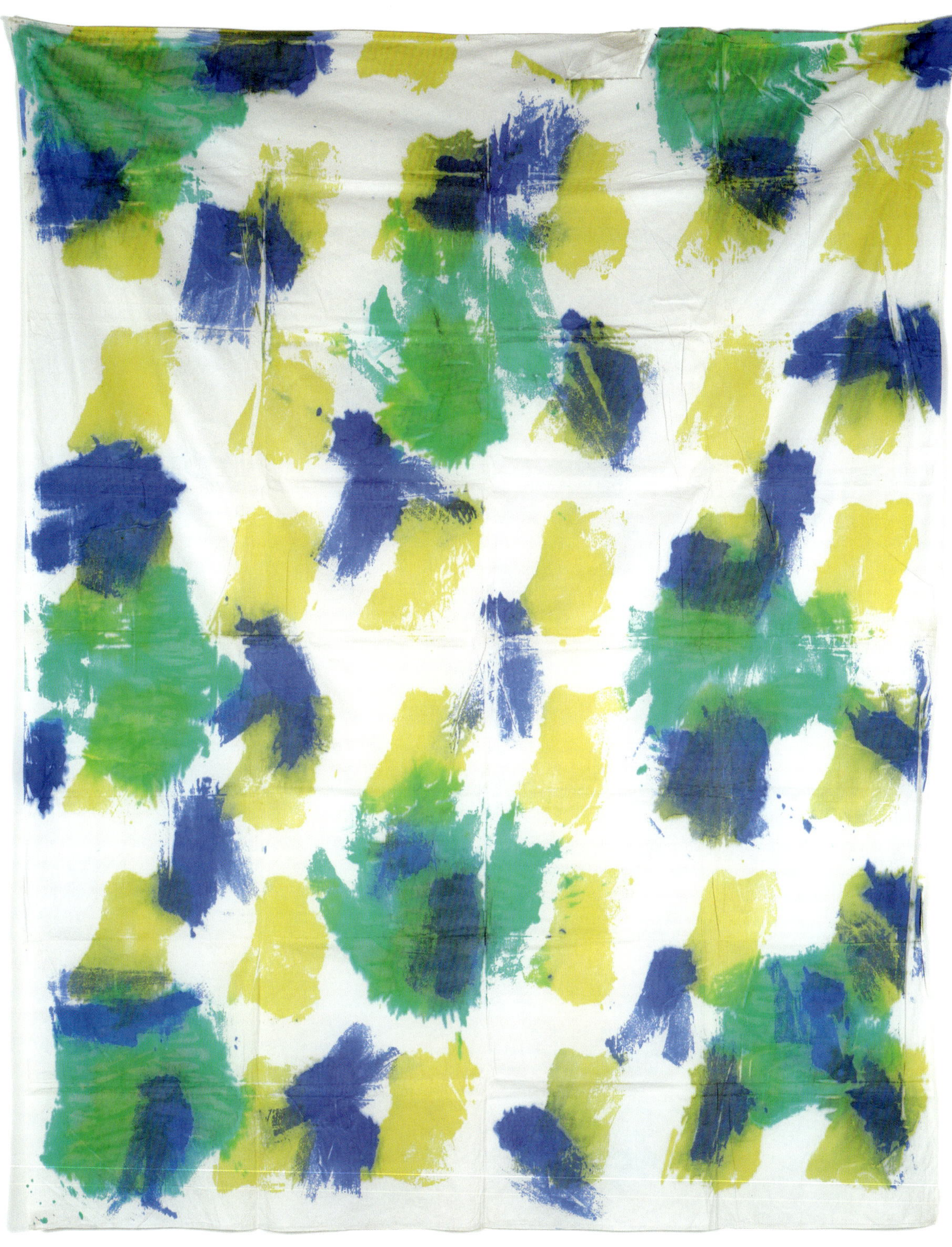

Lee Ufan

CORRESPONDANCE

1997

acrylic on canvas

89 ⅜ × 71 ⅝" | 227 × 181.9 cm

Claude Viallat

Our time argues with us

without giving us any arguments,

could it be that it is lying

even leaving us hanging?

Turning over a new page

without worrying about time

could be a possible ladder

to climb for a while

to go unconsciously toward spiritual paths

with no known direction.

Turn around.

Look behind you into the meanderings of memory to extract from what will become the derisory grail of tomorrow.

This miniscule, hackneyed idea, which will remain an unanswered question for a while.

If I walk without progressing, I progress without walking.

In recent paintings, I have worked on a number of folded canvases attached end-to-end. The geometry of the fabrics stuck together plays with the external shape of the canvas and the shapes that cover it, often following the folds and the empty spaces created within the painting that accompany the painted sections.

All these elements punctuate a relatively random surface, visible from all sides, with the meaning given to the painted shapes, without a clear horizon line, neither top nor bottom, nor any possibility of top or bottom, bringing the canvas back to its position on the floor during creation, accessible from all sides: Another way of perceiving it "among others" and demystifying it. Its materiality, the play of colors and shapes, remains the emerging force that the painting creates on the wall.

Uncertain, indecisive glances, made sometimes uneasy by the complication of angles and lines, as well as the scansion of colors.

Instead of an affirmation, it offers a point of view.

The whole being created by the accumulation of multiple points of view.

Presenting the work, positioning it and repositioning it, confronting its detail and its mass, organizing possible relationships, movement of views and ideas, unimagined aesthetic shocks resulting from encounters or gazes giving rise to what it could become, is its primary interest.

It opens up a multiplicity of readings and reflections, potential future states, and a memory of all the positions that have already existed.

A continuum in the logical implementation of the totality of the work.

Take the shape in all directions, remove its simple verticality to generalize it in possible positions, see it fragmented or whole, and accept its raw existence in its materialities, know it and recognize it, impose it or inform it as pictorial truth, a threshold of formal and spiritual visibility.

The folded, unfolded, loose canvas exists and hits us when, laid flat, we recognize it and place all our concerns, inventions, projections, and future or past sources of interest in it.

It opens up a number of potential perspectives and pending plans open to reflection, sending us back to our verticality, to the ground and to the walls of the cave where the first hand was placed, opening up art to representation.

Demystifying painting, bringing it back to its constituent elements: material, color, surface, and the intuitive geometry that they create, multiple open readings, isolated codes that fill and spiritualize it, offerings for communication and relationships between individuals who personalize the presumed meanings attributed or given to it.

Open to the senses, beginning with the repetitive silence of a random shape, a great presumption.

If in the 1970s the installation and workspace for Supports/Surfaces was recognized, and if over the years its interest was genuine, it is because all the paintings that were cultivated and reworked were the result of questioning and a profound need.

All the information about the craft is with us and in front of us as potential questions.

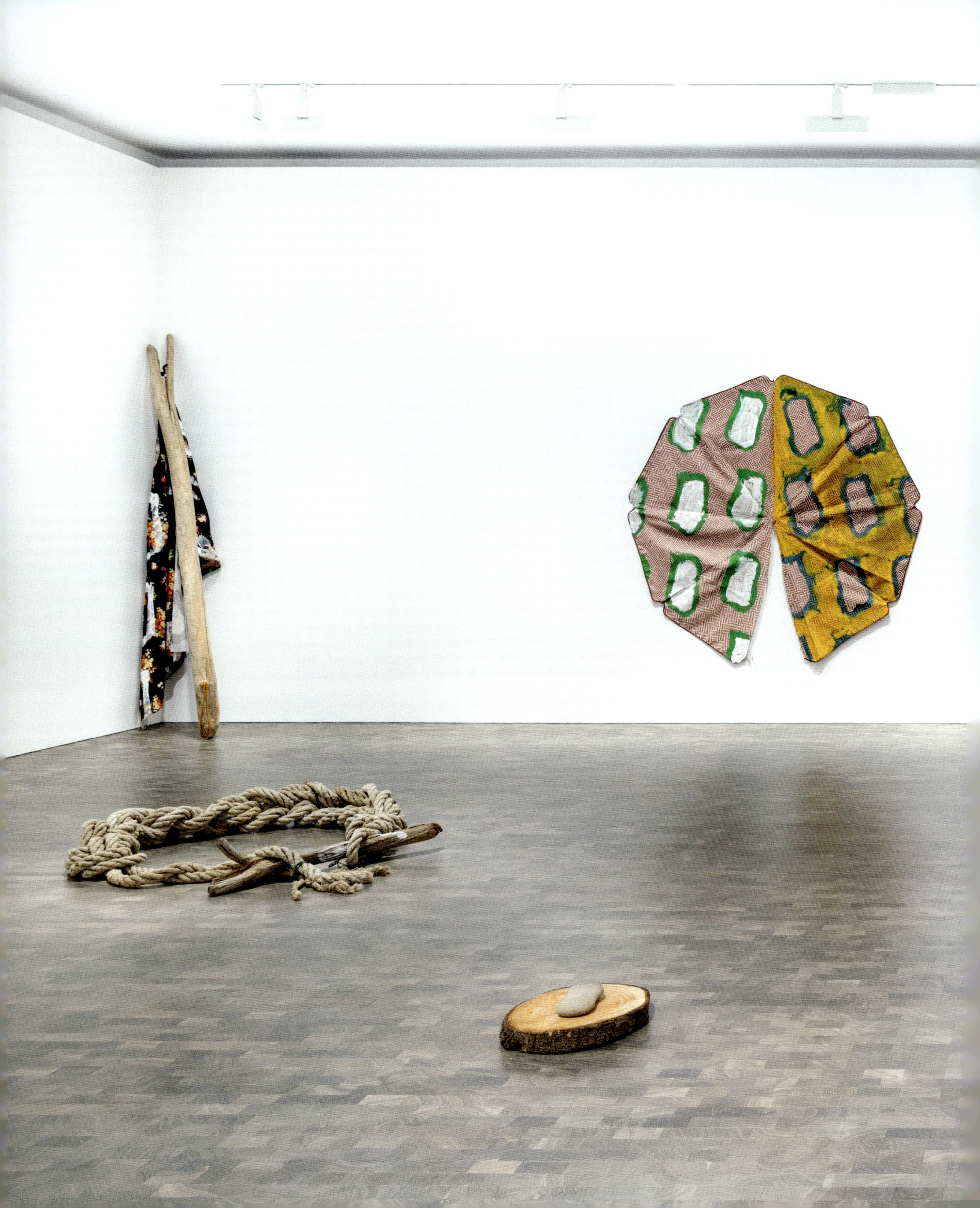

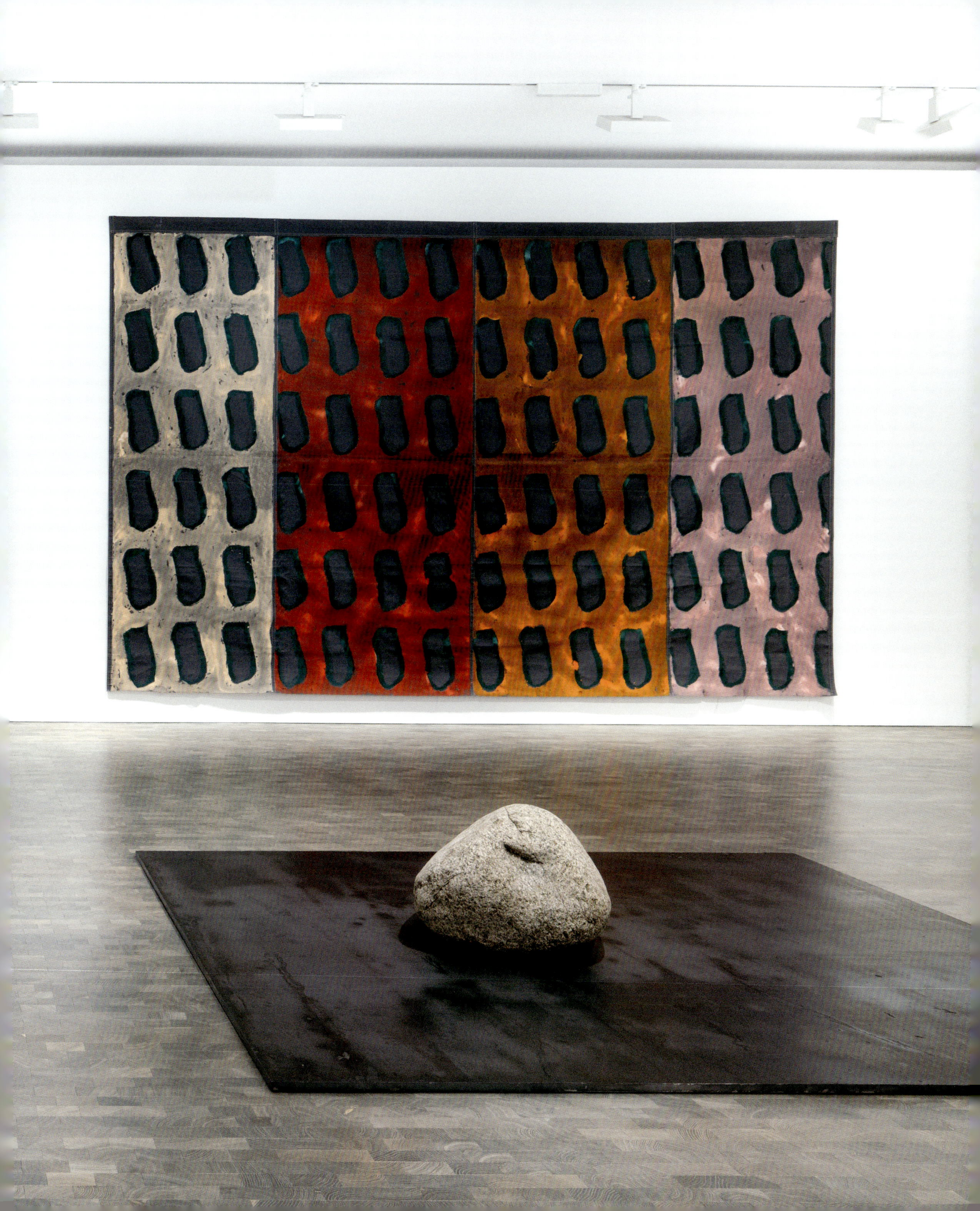

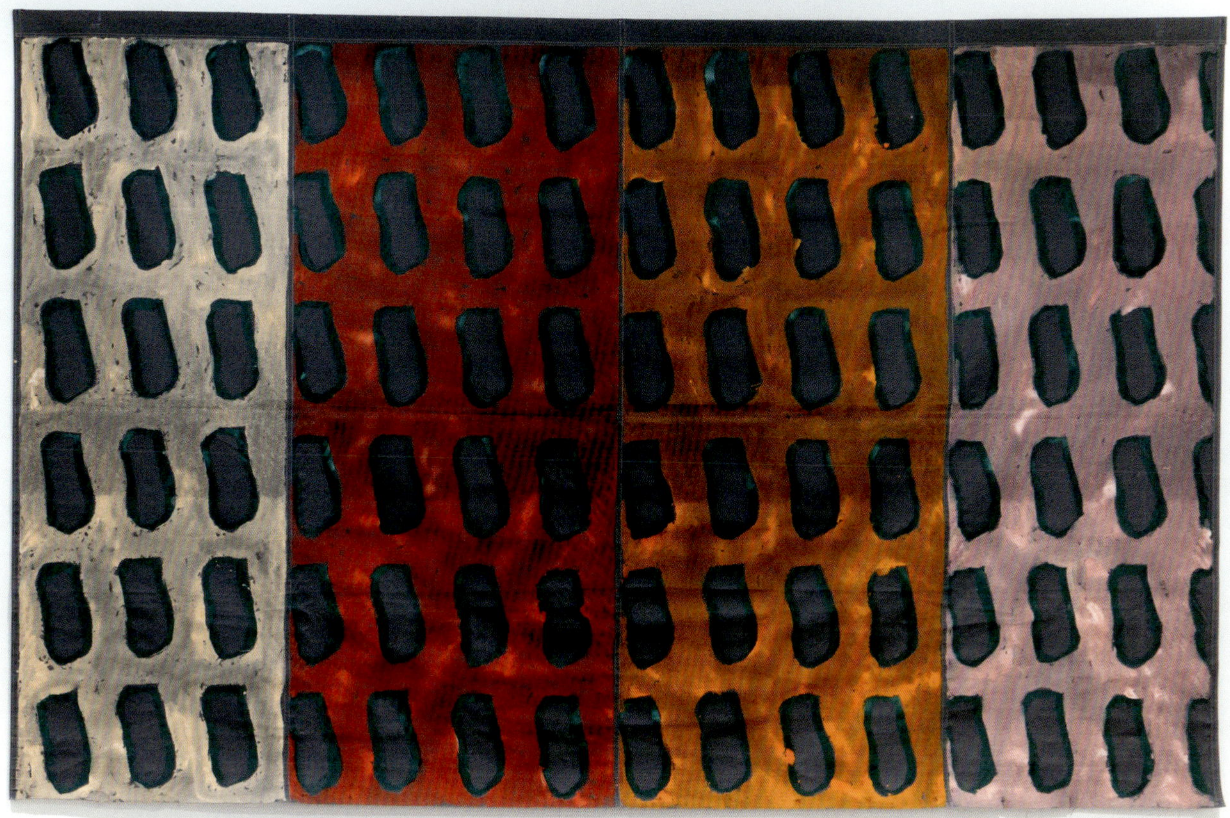

LEE UFAN

23 **RELATUM**
1968/2023
glass and stone
glass 110 ¼ × 98 7/16 × 13/16" | 280 × 250 × 2.1 cm
stone 23 ⅝ × 15 ¾ × 15 ¾" | 60 × 40 × 40 cm

24 **FROM POINT**
1977
acrylic on canvas
5 canvases, each 1 15/16 × 15 ¾" | 5 × 40 x 3 cm
overall 1 15/16 × 79 ¼ × 1 3/16" | 5 × 201.3 × 3 cm

25 **FROM LINE**
1977
acrylic on canvas
5 canvases, each 15 ¾ × 1 15/16" | 40 × 4.9 x 3 cm
overall 15 ¾ × 25 9/16 × 1 3/16" | 40 × 65 × 3 cm

26 **RELATUM — THE ROPE DRAIN**
1974/2023
rope and nails
dimensions variable

27 **RELATUM**
1977/2023
cotton and wire
dimensions variable

30 **RELATUM — THINGS AND WORDS**
1969/2023
canvas
3 canvases, each 118 ⅛ × 78 ¾" | 300 × 200 cm

64 **RESPONSE**
2023
acrylic on canvas
89 ⅜ × 71 ⅝" | 227 × 182 cm

65 **RESPONSE**
2023
acrylic on canvas
89 ⅜ × 71 ⅝" | 227 × 182 cm

69 **CORRESPONDANCE**
1992
acrylic on canvas
89 ⅜ × 71 ⅝" | 227 × 181.9 cm

76 **RELATUM — THE POSITION**
1990/2023
steel and stone
steel plate 94 ½ × 74 13/16 × 13/16" | 240 × 190 × 2 cm
stone 27 9/16 × 23 5/8 × 19 11/16" | 70 × 60 × 50 cm

86 **CORRESPONDANCE**
1997
acrylic on canvas
89 ⅜ × 71 ⅝" | 227 × 181.9 cm

CLAUDE VIALLAT

41 **1975/028**
1975
mordant dye on canvas
98 ⅜ × 78 ¾" | 249.9 × 200 cm

45 **1973/003**
1973
carbonyl on fabric
117 5/16 × 83 ½" | 298 × 212.1 cm

46 **1975/016**
1975
acrylic on two canvases stitched together
110 ¼ × 82 11/16" | 280 × 210 cm

49 **1977/054**
1977
acrylic on circular canvas
diameter 92 ½" | 235 cm

50 **1977/024**
1977
acrylic on fragment of tent with window made of insect mesh
106 5/16 × 83 ⅞" | 270 × 213 cm

53 **1973/026**
1973
mordant dye on fabric
99 ⅝ × 78 ¾" | 253 × 200 cm

55 **1987/OB005**
1987
rope and driftwood assemblage
70 ⅞ × 11 13/16 × 19 11/16" | 180 × 30 × 50 cm

56 **1975/023**
1975
acrylic on fabric exposed to rain
90 9/16 × 82 11/16" | 230 × 210 cm

70 **2022/OB018 — TRIBUTE TO LEE UFAN**
2022
wood and pebble assemblage
diameter 13 ¾" | 34.9 cm

70 **2020/OB026**
2020
acrylic on wood and string
39 ⅜ × 31 ½" | 100 × 80 cm

71 **2023/OB020**
2023
driftwood and acrylic on fabric
96 ⅞ × 5 ⅞" | 246.1 × 14.9 cm

73 **2022/124**
2022
acrylic on butted fabrics
66 ⅛ × 77 3/16" | 168 × 196.1 cm

75 **2022/119**
2022
acrylic on butted fabrics
35 13/16 × 76" | 91 × 193 cm

78 **2022/115**
2022
acrylic on fabric
71 ¼ × 50 13/16" | 181 × 129.1 cm

79 **2022/138**
2022
acrylic on butted fabrics
69 5/16 × 40 9/16" | 176.1 × 103 cm

83 **2022/184**
2022
acrylic on parasol canvas
diameter 68 ⅞" | 174.9 cm

85 **1974/027**
1974
mordant dye on white sheet
109 7/16 × 81 ½" | 278 × 207 cm

Published on the occasion of
LEE UFAN AND CLAUDE VIALLAT
ENCOUNTER
JUNE 2 – JULY 29, 2023

Pace Gallery
5 Hanover Square
London

Cover: *Lee Ufan and Claude Viallat: Encounter*, Pace London

Photography:
Photo Courtesy Castelli Gallery: p. 16
Cyrille Cauvet: pp. 41–43, 45–46, 49–50, 53, 55–56, 70–71, 73, 75, 78–79, 83, 85
Michel Delluc: pp. 8, 11
Damian Griffiths: cover, pp. 2–3, 6–7, 20–21, 23–32, 38–39, 62–67, 69, 76–77, 80–81, 86, 92–93
Ella Kilford: p. 58
© Studio Lee Ufan: pp. 10, 37
© Studio Lee Ufan / Photo by Claire Dorn: p. 19
Courtesy of the Nobuo Sekine Estate and Blum & Poe, Los Angeles/New York/Tokyo: p. 15
Courtesy Atelier de Claude Viallat: p. 61

Creative Director: Tomo Makiura
Design: Tomo Makiura and Alexis Liebes
Production: Paul Pollard
Editorial Director: Gillian Canavan
Editorial Manager: Madeline Gilmore
Rights & Reproductions: Vincent Wilcke
Color Separations: Altaimage, New York

Typeset in GT Pressura and Calluna
Printing: Meridian Printing, East Greenwich, Rhode Island

ISBN: 978-1-948701-65-5
Library of Congress Control Number: 2023938483
Available through ARTBOOK | D.A.P.
75 Broad Street, Suite 630 New York, NY 10004
www.artbook.com